T'AI CHI CHI
CH'UAN

This book is dedicated to my wife, Susan, who is showing as much aptitude as a t'ai chi beginner as she had patience with me while I "gave birth" to this manuscript.

It is also dedicated to all those practitioners and instructors who continue both the traditions and the evolution of our art.

T'AI CHI CH'UAN

THE MARTIAL SIDE

MICHAEL BABIN

PALADIN PRESS
BOULDER, COLORADO

T'ai Chi Ch'uan:
  The Martial Side
by Michael Babin

Copyright © 1992 by Michael Babin

ISBN 0-87364-679-7
Printed in the United States of America

Published by Paladin Press, a division of
Paladin Enterprises, Inc., P.O. Box 1307,
Boulder, Colorado 80306, USA.
(303) 443-7250

Direct inquiries and/or orders to the above address.

PALADIN, PALADIN PRESS, and the "horse head" design
are trademarks belonging to Paladin Enterprises and
registered in the United States Patent and Trademark Office.

CONTENTS

Michael Babin *cares* for his students. This, to me, is the first sign of a good teacher. This attitude shows in his classes: a beaming, genuine smile and verbal exclamations when someone gets something right.

Michael has learned from a number of well-respected teachers, and over the years he has worked out how to share this knowledge. This book is one way of sharing that gained knowledge and has been written with a genuine need to give out the "good oil." Rest assured that this book is no mystical load of mumbo-jumbo, but rather good, practical knowledge given for all of the right reasons.

Erle Montaigue
Master Degree,
World Taiji
Boxing Association

FOREWORD

太極拳

I hope the many talented and dedicated women practicing t'ai chi ch'uan will forgive me for the predominant use of masculine pronouns in parts of the text. I am being "sexist" only to avoid overusing awkward phrases like "his/her."

As the functional side of t'ai chi depends on defensive tactics, sensitivity, skill refinement, and intuition rather than on aggression, size, and strength, it is a pity that more women do not approach t'ai chi to answer their needs for martial/self-defense skills.

Those who train properly benefit accordingly. I remember Mireille, a tiny, fifty-year-old native of France, who had the uncanny ability to kick her male partners in the crotch no matter what tactic they tried to use on her. She always looked mildly embarrassed at such success, but it didn't stop her from denting many an athletic cup (and the occasional ego).

Sadly, it seems that many t'ai chi classes are composed almost exclusively of women who are there primarily to learn form. Conversely, those few

OF INTEREST TO WOMEN

teachers and clubs that emphasize the interactive or martial side of the art are almost exclusively composed of men, despite the fact that women are learning martial arts and self-defense in ever-increasing numbers.

It is my hope that the following pages will help motivate more women to learn the martial side of the art to complete their understanding of its practice and teaching.

This is a primer in the sense that it is a small introductory book on selected aspects of t'ai chi ch'uan.

My hope is that a new perspective may suit the needs of a particular group of t'ai chi practitioners—those with an intermediate level of skill who are interested in the martial side of the art as well as in its solo aspects.

There are many books aimed at beginners, and in all honesty, it is difficult to teach yourself any of this martial exercise's physical aspects from even the best-written and most completely illustrated text.

Unless you're very talented or have a great deal of related martial experience, you can no more develop a real feel for t'ai chi from a book (even this one!) than you can easily build a home after having purchased a set of floor plans, lumber, and tools. Good intentions are necessary for any worthwhile endeavor, but they do not replace skill and experience.

A picture may well be worth a thousand words but *not* when it comes to teaching mental/spiritual attitudes or martial techniques whose value is real-

INTRODUCTION

ized by movement and intuition as opposed to static posing and physical reflex.

However, books are of some use as learning tools for those who already have an experiential framework to which they can relate new material. In addition, books can be used to learn about aspects of training of which you were unaware. After all, if you don't know there is such a thing as da-lu, how can you decide whether or not you want or need to practice it?

Consequently, this text is aimed at those who have learned and practiced one or more forms and are wondering about new directions for their training. It is also aimed at those who have studied some of the martial aspects of the art (e.g., classical push-hands) and are wondering how they can deepen their martial skill.

Over the last six years, some of my students have been kind enough to suggest that they have gained the occasional insight from reading my published articles on various aspects of the practice of yang-style t'ai chi. Consequently, for better and for worse, revisions of those articles form the core of this book.

My own particular interest is the interactive, martial side of t'ai chi ch'uan, and if such prejudices tend to show in my writings, that is only to be expected.

As the text is aimed primarily at those with previous t'ai chi experience, I have assumed that the reader is already familiar with its literary classics (which define the art no matter which variation of it you study) and the jargon of Taoism and t'ai chi. I make no apology for failing to define them once again.

The study of t'ai chi ch'uan, like the study of one of its roots, Taoism, is a lifelong immersion in a sea of questions. Asking relevant questions is both a source of frustration and enlightenment. Seeming to answer one question may well lead you to discover further questions whose existence or relevance to your training you had not previously suspected.

This learning process is full of contrasts, pitfalls, ambiguities, and a simplicity seemingly obscured with detail and controversy over which style, which teacher, is the most competent.

Unfortunately, North American t'ai chi in particular has assumed a pseudospiritual veneer from its contact with the New Age movement, which is more than a little at odds with its rough and unromantic Chinese beginnings. It is important to remember that these training methods were developed by pragmatic men who were determined to "do unto others before they had it done unto them!"

This romanticizing of the art has resulted in the tendency of many Western adherents to ignore or obscure its martial roots. Many have also blithely confused skill and/or understanding with collecting knowledge primarily for the sake of accumulation.

In this way, the overly intellectual confuse theoretical understanding with buying (but not always studying) a library of books on t'ai chi and its related disciplines. Conversely, the overly physical think they can absorb its principles and tactics by superficially learning a variety of forms from different styles.

Sadly, books are only of use if they are both well-written and well-studied. Form training is only of use if your feel for each pattern is an "internal" one and not just a case of technical mastery. A few talented individuals can profit by learning a multitude of forms, but most of us should settle for one or two that become as much a part of us as the ability to use a stairway without thinking about the process of which foot goes next!

I neither speak nor read Chinese and have no pretensions of being a scholar in terms of the history and theory behind t'ai chi ch'uan or Taoism. However, neither fault (and my wife assures me that I have others) has kept me from coming to a variety of conclusions about the practice and teaching of t'ai chi.

In particular, I will discuss some of the controversial areas of its study from a variety of perspectives—not just my own or a specialized ideology. In addition, I will, in general, discuss concepts and approaches rather than training specifics. These are best learned under the personal guidance of an experienced instructor.

Those individuals who are contemplating learning t'ai chi, are looking for a picture book of postures and techniques, have just begun its practice, or have no interest in the martial arts may well find some of my comments confusing, irrelevant, or irritating, but that too can stimulate the learning process.

You won't always agree with my statements, but even the process of disagreement can help you to see more clearly your position on different t'ai chi issues. In some ways, I've learned almost as much from instructors I disagreed with or disliked as I have from those who inspired me by their personalities as well as their skill.

The following pages are based on my understanding and application of the history, philosophy, theory, and tactics, both physical and mental, as learned from a variety of teachers—in particular Allan Weiss of Canada; Erle Montaigue of Australia; and William C.C. Chen of New York.

To these talented and dedicated instructors, I offer my thanks for sharing their expertise and goodwill and for being such fine role models for "junior" instructors like myself.

Any errors or oversimplifications in the text are my own doing, and the blame should hardly be laid at their feet, even if they were generous enough to accept it!

Hopefully, the following pages can, in some small way, become thought-provoking in the best sense of that phrase.

Chapter One, **Defining the Topic**, describes the art within a philosophical and historical context and suggests why and how its study can be approached.

Chapter Two, **Choosing a Style and Instructor**, discusses the different forms and styles available and gives suggestions on how to find an instructor who is both competent and compatible with your needs.

Chapter Three, **Learning How to Learn**, touches on the mental attitudes necessary for learning in general and t'ai chi in particular.

Chapter Four, **Solo Form: Foundation of T'ai Chi**, describes the key physical, emotional, and intellectual aspects of form practice.

Chapter Five, **Ch'i for Healing and Combat,** discusses the concept of internal energy from a pragmatic viewpoint with particular reference to ch'i-kung, sexual energy, and the martial use of ch'i.

Chapter Six, **Martial Fundamentals**, discusses the "thirteen postures," push-hands, and da-lu, as well as the role of rooting, uprooting, sticking, and pushing in achieving competence in the interactive exercises that form the basis of future martial skill.

Chapter Seven, **T'ai Chi Self-Defense Part One: Core Concepts**, covers the training methods and attitudes that help you learn to apply the fundamentals in a defensive manner.

Chapter Eight, **T'ai Chi Self-Defense Part Two: Maximizing Your Training**, covers more advanced concepts, including sparring, using safety gear, and training for unarmed defense against weapons.

Chapter Nine, **T'ai Chi and Martial Cross-Training**, discusses the potential value of cross-training in martial arts that are compatible with the principles of t'ai chi.

Finally, if I may refer to my comment about t'ai chi being a sea of questions: if you despair of reaching the far shore, you'll give up prematurely and swim back to security, or despair and sink into the abyss when exhausted.

You must learn to pace yourself and, while keeping your eyes on the distant shore, allow yourself to experience the pleasure (and effort) of each stroke. I hope the following pages help that voyage.

T'ai chi ch'uan (also spelled tai chi chuan and, more recently, Taijiguan in English) has become increasingly popular in the Western world in the last few decades.

For some, it is a gentle solo exercise that aids relaxation, is a form of meditation, and improves health; for others, it has recently become a sport in which students compete in push-hands or demonstrate excellence of form execution at local and international events; and, for a minority, it is also a self-defense system that can be effectively practiced into middle age and beyond.

The three Chinese characters are traditionally, and to Western ears somewhat arrogantly, translated as "Supreme Ultimate Boxing."

The first two words refer to the "Supreme Ultimate" or "Grand Terminus," a philosophical concept which is usually depicted as the famous black and white symbol associated both with t'ai chi ch'uan and the "Tao." The latter word is often translated, not completely accurately, as "Nature."

CHAPTER 1

DEFINING THE TOPIC

Each color of the symbol may also be shown as containing a small spot of its opposite, which signifies that there are no complete extremes in nature. For example, hard (yang/white or red/masculine/penetrating/heaven) should always have the essence of soft (yin/black or green/feminine/receptive/earth) within its substance and vice versa.

When this balancing process fails, an individual loses internal and external harmony, and this, in turn, has both personal and social ramifications.

Being overly yang manifests itself in specific physical and emotional illnesses, for example, being obsessed with the desire to accumulate possessions and accomplishments, no matter what the social or individual cost. Being overly yin reveals itself in different physical and/or emotional health problems, for example, being overly timid or withdrawn.

In martial terms, yin and yang refer to the balancing of such energies for self-defense, both in terms of improving your health and preventing others from harming it, through specific training methods. These are as concerned with the mind and spirit of the practitioner as his or her body. T'ai chi and related martial arts are referred to as "internal" arts for this reason.

The third Chinese character, though literally meaning "fist," is often translated as "boxing" and refers as much to self-cultivation as to martial skills. In recent years, there have been suggestions that it would be less grandiose and more accurate in martial terms to translate t'ai chi ch'uan as "yin and yang boxing."

TAOISM AND T'AI CHI

While t'ai chi's evolution was influenced in part by Buddhism (especially the ch'an school, a Chinese blend of Indian Buddhism and native Taoist thought), its roots are firmly in Taoism. Consequently, before going further in defining t'ai chi, we should take a brief and tantalizing (in the sense of enticing you to do more research) look at the latter topic.

In terms of its philosophical form, Taoism was defined primarily by books attributed to two men, Lao Tzu and Chuang Tzu, in the fourth century, B.C. In strict scholarly terms it is very difficult to identify whether these two were historical figures or whether their respective books were written by one or more unknown authors.

Lao Tzu may be the most famous of the two, but it is important to remember that the principles (i.e., the interplay of yin and yang) emphasized in the book he supposedly wrote, *Tao Te Ching*, had long been an intrinsic part of Chinese culture. For example, the unknown author(s) and commentator(s) who created the text on internal energy cultivation and medicine, *The Nei Ching* (usually entitled *The Yellow Emperor's Classic of Internal Medicine* in English), had used the same concepts hundreds of years before Lao Tzu and Chuang Tzu.

In any case, the early Taoist writings advocate returning to a simplicity of life-style, inner and social tranquility, living in accordance with the rhythms of nature, and "wu-wei," which means "nonaction" or "noninterference."

The Taoistic sense of nonaction has frequently been superficially understood by those elements of society that prefer to interpret Taoism either as a rationalization for doing whatever you want or as a rejection of the world of the senses. My feeling is that wu-wei is not a rejection of the emotions or the need for human interdependence, but rather an intuitive maturity which accepts and adapts to the sometimes good, sometimes bad nature of daily life. For the early Taoists, life wasn't a question of existence versus nonexistence or right versus wrong. Instead, they saw it in organic terms of self-sufficiency and advocated the value of relativity in terms of determining social values.

To understand this approach to living, it is important to know that Taoism sprang out of a very turbulent era in Chinese history: a generations-long period of internal warfare between a kaleidoscope of states whose rulers were more concerned with conquering each other than serving the needs of their citizens. Then, as now, such warfare went hand-in-hand with treachery, massacre, famine, pestilence, and religious ferment.

It shouldn't be too hard to understand, then, why some would advocate and others would be attracted to a philosophy that seemed to suggest withdrawal from the perils and strife of daily life in favor of a simple, contemplative existence.

In martial terms, living in such tumultuous times would certainly explain why the Taoists were obliged to create and practice methods of personal self-defense to augment those exercises designed solely for health and spiritual purposes.

While other Chinese thinkers were more concerned with human relations, social propriety, and improving political systems, the Taoists were content to use allegory and humor to expose the futility and hypocrisy of trying to rule others without first knowing how to rule yourself. In addition, they advised their listeners to understand the futility of imposing human concepts of order on nature.

Human beings are, by nature, conservative and resistant to change, which is perhaps why Taoism as a philosophy has rarely been accepted by large numbers of people—as it is built on the necessity of embracing the validity and cyclical nature of change as a means of understanding life both on an individual and cosmic basis.

In China, society and the extended family unit has always been more important than its individual members. Accordingly, Communists and Confucians, though their formal theories are quite different, are alike in depending on a rigidly centralized state and subservience of the needs of the individual to those of the state. Neither system does more than tolerate individualists, and both are quick to dismiss them as eccentric.

The Taoist philosophers gently mocked rigidity and pomposity in all its forms and were, by and large, ignored or treated with suspicion by the ruling class—unless their skills were needed. They were better received by the common people, but, for that level of society, the philosophy was less influential than the mystical and superstitious side of Taoism.

This very ambiguity is part of the reason these early Taoists are so intriguing to modern Westerners. It is also important to remember that our perception of Taoism can't help but be colored by our own emotional needs. It is easy to romanticize the early Taoists, but they are gone and can no more be re-created than their essential social context, old China. Such modern tendencies can be minimized, if not eliminated, so that we don't force the limited historical records to suit our own preconceptions and emotional needs.

On the other hand, the present popularity of philosophical Taoism (there are, for example, dozens of different translations of the *Tao Te Ching* into English alone) lies partly in this very vagueness! You can interpret most of its key passages in many different ways—and how you do so will depend on your personality and prejudices. Having said this, it is also important to note that striving for absolute objectivity is also immaterial to the validity of your approach to modern Taoism—as a philosophy it is built on change and adaptability.

My interpretation of early Taoism suggests that the best of these philosophers were much like *my* favorite Western "Taoist," the character played by Anthony Quinn in the movie *Zorba the Greek*.

I'm not sure that I like Zorba, but at the same time he is someone for whom you grow, almost despite yourself, to care about. You know where you stand with such an individual; whether you want his honesty or not, it is there—like that of a child.

Zorba has that quality prized by the Taoists of old: "tzu-jan" or "self-so." He is a natural man who experiences his life in a way that is free of emotional restriction and social convention. Some of his actions are reprehensible and selfish by social norms, but, at the same time, you can see that he is acting simply and spontaneously, not from malice. If he can be accused of anything, it is a lack of forethought. However, this very lack of planning is, in itself, very Taoistic. In addition, he has a natural and "earthy" sense of humor and an appreciation of the value of movement to the body and emotions.

Being Greek, Zorba receives his emotional and physical release from dance, but his appreciation of its holistic value is truly Taoistic. In one moving scene, he has just danced himself into exhaustion on the beach and tells his English friend in whispered gasps that he did the same thing the night that his firstborn son died.

"He was only three," Zorba whispers. "It was only the dancing that kept me from going mad with grief, even though the others thought I'd gone crazy." Lao Tzu and Chuang Tzu would have understood his apparent lack of propriety.

When talking about later Taoism, it is also important to remember that it was influenced, over the centuries, by

Buddhism and Confucianism and diverged along a variety of paths: the hygienic concepts of the so-called Five Elements theorists; traditional Chinese medicine; theories and practices of sexual mysticism; a complex folklore of religious superstition; the need for martial skills for personal defense and to resist upperclass repression and foreign invaders; and a search for physical as well as spiritual immortality that included alchemic practices, the use of breath control, and magic potions.

The later Taoists were concerned primarily with the cultivation of ch'i (intrinsic life energy). They believed that by living a simple existence away from society and in touch with nature, especially in mountainous regions where there were more likely to be mists (believed to be the earth's ch'i), they would be able to learn to store, concentrate, and transform such vital energies for a variety of purposes. For these men, the main aim was to prolong their natural life span and even, under the right conditions, become immortal. The legends and written histories of t'ai chi abound with stories of Taoist hermits whose existential and spiritual development was mirrored by their martial skills so that they seemed almost superhuman.

One such individual, Chang San-feng, was reputed (in at least some of the accounts of his life) to have created the original thirteen postures of t'ai chi as a result of a dream. A pragmatist might also feel that this creative process was more likely an intuitive blend of the tactics Chang had observed in a fight between a crane and a snake with his own knowledge of traditional Chinese medicine and martial techniques.

Whether or not Chang and other Taoistic martial artists are mythical is largely immaterial to what t'ai chi is today. However, the overly intellectual side of the art is well-characterized by those practitioners and scholars who research the sometimes forged and often contradictory oral and written records in an effort to discover its true roots.

The search for those roots is often carried to obsessive lengths. When one reads the various interpretations of the t'ai chi records, it soon becomes obvious, if nothing else does, that correct lineage seems very important to many practitioners. Unfortunately, this preoccupation with who is doing genuine as opposed to false t'ai chi is more indicative of the mind-set of the most vocal critics than of the relative worth of the various styles and approaches currently available.

This is due to the incomplete and often contradictory nature of the historical records that have survived and to the Chinese tendency (often done in good faith) to ascribe an elaborate genealogy to new concepts or practices. Chinese society valued the old, not the innovator.

I suspect that this need to know who is teaching "original" or "authentic" t'ai chi has more to do with the emotional needs of those who need to feel superior by way of their dogmatic adherence to the teachings of a recognized expert. That said, it is also important to have some idea as to whether or not the t'ai chi you are proposing to learn is valid. A particular instructor's approach is not necessarily better just because he can trace it back five generations; however, if it has survived that long, it must have some legitimacy—especially for those styles which have retained the martial applications.

In any case, the principles and tactics that were later to evolve into the present main styles of t'ai chi ch'uan came from the union of Taoist concepts with a variety of existing martial/hygienic practices. This process can be partially traced to the present day from the beginning of the twentieth century and, with a much larger margin of error, back to the beginning of the Manchu Dynasty in the mid-1600s.

T'AI CHI CH'UAN TODAY

Like the Tao, the reality of t'ai chi is best described by stating that which it is not.

Body Work

It is not a method of spontaneous or choreographed physical movement like dance. Rather, when taught properly, it is a series of postures linked formally and/or spontaneously and performed slowly to balance energy flow and internal health, increase lower body strength, and improve balance, flexibility, and eye-hand coordination, while developing a sense of personal integrity in terms of rhythm and movement.

It is not a means of posture and structural reintegration like the Alexander Method. Instead, for those who suffer physical ills brought on by bad habits, it is a means of realizing how the effects of poor posture can, over the long term, contribute to problems such as chronic back and neck/shoulder pain. The intent is to become aware of your physical state so that, over time, you *encourage* rather than *force* good posture.

It is not a means of learning to relax like the discipline of yoga. Rather, for the tense individual, it is a means of learning to observe how the body responds to the stress of self-observation and to learning new things and how the mind/body can be *allowed* to release muscle tension so that only the right amount of energy is used to do the work of the moment.

It is not a cure-all for a wide variety of physical and emotional ailments like homeopathic medicine or physiotherapy. But it has very real therapeutic uses when done properly over the long term.

Many practitioners, and the medical researchers of China, also believe that the proper practice of the solo form can beneficially stimulate the nervous system through its ch'i pathways for healing purposes. It does so through physical and, on a more subtle level, psychological training. Such effort can lead the student, who is emotionally ready to be led, to understand him/herself in order to lessen the negative influences of modern life (e.g., insufficient exercise, pollution, stress, poor diet).

Spiritual and Emotional Considerations

It is not a superior way of life transplanted from another culture. Instead, for the North American who feels alienated from his own culture, it can be a way of seeing how borrowing from other cultures can be a way of changing Western approaches to daily life without mindlessly embracing a discipline that is, in many ways, mythic even in its country of origin.

It is not a means of meditation like Zen. Rather, for the intellectual, it is a means of learning how absurdly active the mind can be and how easily we can become separated from our emotional and physical selves.

The Western tradition encourages the definition and classification of all things, even the spiritual. T'ai chi, on the other hand, emphasizes that each of us is an integral part of nature. Its study allows the mind/body to learn how to experience itself holistically.

Such meditation has nothing to do with trance states and everything to do with learning to be attentive to yourself and to your environment. It is a form of enhanced awareness of self and of our connection with that energy that defines existence—the breath of God in the Western Christian tradition, ch'i in the Chinese tradition, and the controversial energy patterns of modern quantum physics.

Martial Training

It is not an exotic or mysterious kung-fu fighting system. Instead, for the individual concerned about the need for self-defense skills, it is a way of experiencing the difference between *how* and *why* we perceive danger, both psychological and physical, and how we can most effectively deal, on all levels, with fear and aggression in ourselves and others.

The combative aims are to train the practitioner to react calmly, naturally, and with the appropriate level of force. It also teaches how not to be caught up in fear or the need to respond in predictable tactical ways.

A practitioner is admonished by the classics to strive to internalize the following concept: the mind ("i") commands, muscular strength ("li") obeys, and energy ("ch'i") follows.

THE CLASSIC PRINCIPLES OF T'AI CHI

Balance must be physical and emotional. The spine is upright without being rigid and is allowed to *gently* compress, extend, and spiral from the base of the spine to the crown of the head.

In martial terms, this principle refers to maintaining your balance while under attack, while simultaneously affecting the balance of a training partner or opponent. Effort must be proportional: not too much muscle, not too little; not too much emphasis on one aspect of training to the detriment of others.

Breathing Deeply means learning to breathe so that the

abdomen/torso, not just the upper chest region, expands and contracts. The air is said to be led to the abdomen by the imagination. Once there, the mind aids the biological transformation of oxygen into ch'i, which circulates through the body to improve health and self-defense capabilities—either passively by providing an invisible shield protecting the skin (iron shirt training) or aggressively through "fa-ching," an explosive and concussive transmission of energy.

Concentration involves paying attention to yourself as you practice form and the interactive side of t'ai chi so that all of the principles are in play. This concentration develops an awareness of self and existence that eventually carries over into day-to-day life.

Coordinating and Centering means that the body moves (or does not move) as one. This takes months or years of practice, and mastering its highest level, in which you seemingly disconnect the movement of parts of the body from the movement of the whole, is even more difficult. The mind is coordinated with the body, which is coordinated with the breathing.

Emptiness and Fullness means clearly distinguishing between yin and yang in the body. For example, if the weight is on the left leg, then the other leg should be almost completely weightless. If the lower body is firm and centered, the upper body should be "empty" so that it can yield or neutralize an oncoming force more easily.

However, each must also have a reserve of the opposite energy. For example, when bending the wrist to strike with an open hand, the final posture is not a ninety-degree bend, as this risks injuring the joint. There must remain some yin, some element of flexion, when yang is at its fullest.

Even and Slow refers to developing form movement which (in the yang style at least) is performed in slow motion and with the same tempo throughout, without breaking the postures up into a series of static moments. In terms of the martial function, it refers to a mental and spiritual feeling which transcends the physical need for varying rhythms and speeds when applying your tactics.

Relaxation means that the mind/body/spirit is supple and alive, not just limp and passive. In terms of boxing skills, particular attention must be paid to the waist, shoulders, elbows, and wrists; in health terms, to the lower back and the internal organs as that is where most people accumulate tension from poor posture, laziness, and habitual tension.

Rooting/Sinking means learning to bend the knees to lower the body's center of gravity while lowering your psychic attention from the head or chest to that point just above the hip joints. Once you have accomplished this in your training, it is very difficult for you to lose your balance, even if you are obliged to move suddenly or it is affected adversely by someone else. While rooting means developing the ability to be immobile, this immobility must be "lively," in that you can move easily, if necessary, without compromising your root.

Balance and Change

At the risk of implying a metaphysical side to what was and still is a system of developing good health and martial skills, at its best, t'ai chi is, initially, a structured way of learning to see who and how you are in relation to yourself and those you interact with (i.e., society). Having done this, you learn in time to create a climate that allows you to appreciate and eventually embrace the importance of balance and change.

Creating balance is the crux of the art. When doing form, you gradually realize why your old physical sense of balance was inappropriate, if it was, and improve it while developing a lower, more stable center of gravity. When doing the interactive or martial aspects of the art, you learn how to maintain your own balance while under pressure and how to affect the sense of balance of those with whom you practice, either as a learning tool or to stop aggression.

In addition to balance, t'ai chi is about change. Learning to deal with change as you go from one posture to another in form and learning to deal with the spontaneous and instantaneous changes of push-hands or sparring teach you the importance of relaxing so that your movements are both economical and effective.

In learning such an approach to balance and change, it is necessary to learn to place your trust in *being* as opposed to *becoming*. Most students approach any aspect of the study of t'ai chi with the attitude that they want to improve themselves, learn the necessary related skills, and change their bad habits as much as they can, as fast as they can. Such attitudes, unfortunately, tend to be self-defeating.

Being and becoming, as aspects of yin and yang, can only be reconciled if each, like the famous "double-fish" black and white symbol, contains an element of its opposite.

The scales of t'ai chi, like the rise and fall of the breath, are an eternally shifting interplay that only seem to come to a point of equilibrium before the need for new adjustments arise. As soon as more weight (i.e., new experience) is added to either side, the process of balancing continues.

Resistance to change, like water deprived of flow, brings only stagnation. Similarly, an obsession with being, like most obsessions, tends to detract from balance, which is the cornerstone for understanding the interplay of yin/yang.

True balance can only come from learning to appreciate the inevitability of change and of the need to embrace it as a lifelong process of which you are a part and not an observer.

Balance must be physical, emotional, and intellectual if t'ai chi is to truly be digested as a martial art, a way of personal liberation, and a metaphor of daily life.

Solo Form and Martial Function

Each side of the t'ai chi coin, solo form and martial function, can be practiced by itself with benefit. However, to reap the most benefit, both aspects should be integrated in the same way that we are most integrated as humans when experiencing ourselves as a union of intellect and body, emotion and intellect, rather than as two halves each struggling for preeminence.

While you can derive a great deal of benefit, both physical and mental, from just doing form, deeper progress is very difficult to achieve if you never practice the interactive side of the art—much less the self-defense side.

While doing nothing but form tends to make introspective people even more so; doing nothing but the martial practice tends to make a tense and aggressive person even more so and does nothing to "quiet" him or her.

However, one must also be careful that studying the martial side degenerates into neither a mechanical reliance on the goodwill of a cooperative partner nor a frenzied reliance on force. This is all too likely to happen unless instructor and students alike are diligent.

My own attitude toward the value of the martial side of t'ai chi is that teaching form without function is like giving students a deflated basketball and expecting them to play without hinting at the vital role of air pressure. You may be able to have fun and get some exercise, but don't expect to translate such skills easily if obliged to play with someone who is used to practicing with an inflated ball!

Studying the function as opposed to the form of t'ai chi teaches you to relax in the face of stress and interact in an appropriate, creative, and assertive (not aggressive) manner. Human beings live in societies and need, almost without exception, to learn the skills which allow them to adapt to the changing circumstances of life without being abused, either mentally or physically. T'ai chi is one way of learning such skills.

Let me put it this way: if your understanding is only useful when you are alone and practicing under ideal conditions, can it have *real* mental or physical value? To truly understand yourself from a psychological, integrative perspective, you must train with others.

SUMMARIZING T'AI CHI

My definition of t'ai chi is that it is, in essence, an attitude that is simultaneously vague, due to its deceptive simplicity (the Taoist concepts), and concrete (the principles as laid out in the classics and physical techniques).

Martially, this means that you learn to react spontaneously with tactics that suit the ethical and physical needs of the moment—neither suicidal under-response nor murderous overkill.

Such an attitude may be a sense of frustration if I have difficulty understanding a principle or learning a new posture; it may be the physical and/or emotional pain as I am pushed, punched, thrown, or simply outclassed by another practitioner; it may be the sensual touch of my partner's arms and hands as the two of us practice the interactive, martial side of the art; and, it may be that sublime sense of "oneness" that can come suddenly at some point in my practice when I least expect it.

Even in North America, there are many t'ai chi styles and instructors available. In fact, the noted American internal martial arts practitioner and scholar Robert Smith wrote in one of his excellent books that there seemed to him to be almost as many styles of Chinese boxing as there were instructors!

While this is somewhat of an exaggeration, it is true that unlike the Japanese and Korean martial arts, which tend to be more systematic and cohesive in terms of organizational control, the Chinese arts, including t'ai chi, were and still are (despite the efforts of the Chinese government) characterized by their tendency to evolve according to the creativity, skills, and psychological needs of each instructor.

The process of diversification has certainly not abated with t'ai chi's introduction in North America, home as it is to the cult of individualism.

A quick review of the relevant catalogs offering dozens of books and videos on t'ai chi and related subjects will demonstrate just how popular and varied the

CHAPTER 2

CHOOSING A STYLE AND INSTRUCTOR

art has become in the three decades since it was introduced to North America. In addition, the growing numbers of Western instructors cannot help but bring their own diverse experiences and attitudes to bear on the styles they have learned and, consequently, modify what they, in turn, pass on to their students.

Like all things, this evolutionary process has both good and bad aspects. Doing things the "way that they've always been done" can be as counterproductive as change introduced primarily to suit the needs (and ego) of a particular instructor.

In relation to this process, North American t'ai chi was characterized until recent years by a New Age emphasis on passive relaxation and pseudospiritual concerns. Fortunately, in the last few years a number of teachers have spoken out on the importance of understanding the art's martial side/aspects in order to reap the most benefit from its practice.

Outspoken experts like Dr. Yang Jwing-ming in Boston, Doc Fai-wong in San Francisco, William C.C. Chen in New York, and Erle Montaigue in Australia have, each in their own distinctive manner, demonstrated that separating t'ai chi from its boxing aspect detracts from its value.

Conversely, some traditionalists make a great fuss over maintaining the purity of a style so that what has been taught by the founders remains sacred. In this way, techniques that were invented to fit now outdated theories, tactics, or weapons are retained for all the wrong reasons.

For example, in some Yang-style solo forms, when one does the posture called "Grasp the Needle at the Sea Bottom," the left hand covers the web connecting the thumb and first finger of the right hand. This two-handed grip does give greater leverage, in some ways, for the follow-up downward thrust. However, the hand placement was also originally designed to prevent whomever you had grabbed with your right hand from using a pressure-point attack on the web of that hand to make you let go. As you are unlikely today to be fighting someone who possesses the skill to use such a sophisticated attack, covering a pressure point which is not likely to be threatened in this way limits the tactical use of that posture.

Similarly, a long and somehow exotic pedigree, if such a thing can be proved, does nothing to improve the quality of a particular style or variation of t'ai chi. On the other hand, caring little about what and who came before those practicing today is also symptomatic of attitudes which *may* reduce the art to a preoccupation with innovation, even when such innovation is unnecessary.

As an example of this, some schools of t'ai chi have overemphasized the pushing aspect of its martial aspect—partly to make the practice safer for students and competition and partly because many of the percussive strikes of t'ai chi have been watered down until only the apparent movement is left and not the strike that should have caused that movement.

CHOOSING THE STYLE THAT'S RIGHT FOR YOUR NEEDS

Too much emphasis is put on training with a master, and part of this is due to overt or subconscious racism. Occidentals feel that an instructor should be Oriental, and Chinese students (unless they're second- or third-generation Westerners) will rarely consider learning from a non-Chinese instructor.

Japanese and Korean instructors try to demonstrate the superiority of their martial arts by making them as widespread and standardized as possible. By contrast, the Chinese, until recently, demonstrated their feeling of martial superiority by *not* teaching non-Chinese. Fortunately, there have always been talented exceptions to this rule so that quality instruction has leaked out over the years.

This form of ethnocentrism has declined in the last two decades, although in a minority of t'ai-chi and kung-fu clubs it is still true that Chinese students will get more detailed and effective instruction from a Chinese instructor than non-Chinese students.

This can be explained in part by language barriers in the case of a chief instructor who speaks poor or imperfect English. It doesn't explain the higher fees that non-Chinese students may pay for lower-quality instruction at a few schools.

No matter what his or her race, a master was, and is, someone who "dreamed" as the legendary founder of t'ai chi, Chang Sanfeng, was reputed to have done, of how to improve or adapt what he or she had learned from previous masters and from life.

If I say that t'ai chi could not have been the product of a dream, then I am also saying that no one has the right to modify and develop what has come since. And, if that is valid, what gave Chang San-feng the right to change what he already knew and create t'ai chi?

In the end, whether you choose to study Yang, Chen, Wu, or any of the other t'ai-chi styles will be largely a matter of personal choice and, quite frankly, local availability. Not everyone has the interest, money, or time to travel extensively and regularly to train with someone outside of their immediate geographical area.

Each style has its own fanatics who will claim that their brand of t'ai chi is the "original," the "best for health," the "best for self-defense," the "best for developing ch'i," and so on. However, the truth remains that each style is only as good as the individual instructors within its tradition or organization.

Chen

This style is the original form of t'ai chi and the oldest. It began with Chen Wan-ting at the end of the Ming Dynasty and the beginning of the Manchu Dynasty.

Its forms emphasize both slow and fast, explosive movements, as well as foot- and fist-stamping actions. The energy behind such attacks starts in the waist, transfers down to the foot, and "bounces" from there back up through the spine and out the hands or feet.

It also emphasizes the "Silk-Cocoon Reeling Power" (Chan-Ssu Ching), which can be likened to the expansive and contractile energies of coiling or corkscrewing actions.

There are two main styles of Chen—the "old" and the "new." The old is well-represented by its best-known spokesman in China, Chen Xiaowang, who is a nineteenth-generation descendant of the Chen family in the village of Chenjiagou, where the style originated.

Chen style has become more and more popular in recent years, both in China and the United States, as it has the reputation of being the oldest and the most martial style of t'ai chi. As the forms are powerful, graceful, and dramatic, Chen style is very popular with those interested in the martial applications of t'ai chi and/or form competition.

Yang

This major branch of t'ai chi was founded by Yang Lu-chan in the late nineteenth century. He was the first outsider (not a member of the Chen clan) to learn the style and modified it to suit his previous martial arts training.

While making the movements more expansive and flowing, he still retained fast, explosive actions and athletic kicks in the forms. Subsequent generations of his family, especially his grandson Yang Chen-fu, continued the evolution and spread of the style after his death. Chen-fu made a variety of modifications which, over the decades, softened the outward appearance of the form to emphasize the health aspects as much as the martial aspects in its practice.

The present style is marked by extended and natural movements, the interplay of beautiful postures with subtle power. The Yang "family" styles (of which there are several, depending on which line of Yang Lu-chan's sons is being traced) are similar to, but distinct from, the numerous Yang "styles," which are further modifications done over the last fifty years by a variety of Chinese and non-Chinese instructors.

For example, the numerous (in North America especially) and talented senior students of Ch'eng Man-ching, a senior student of Yang Cheng-fu, have created variations of Cheng's form that are Yang "style" but bear little outward resemblance to what is considered to be orthodox Yang-family-style t'ai chi. In fact, in recent years, there have been suggestions that these instructors should say that they are teaching the Ch'eng style.

Such hairsplitting is extraneous to the inner quality of the t'ai chi skills of instructors like William C.C. Chen and Benjamin Lo. Call it what you like —a rose remains a rose (an apt analogy when you consider that t'ai chi, like a rose, has both great beauty and very sharp thorns).

Another Yang style worthy of note in North America and Europe is that taught by the the Taoist Tai Chi Society. This international association has more than 190 member clubs and began in Canada with the efforts of Master Moy Lin-Shin, originally from Hong Kong. He has devoted his life to spreading his interpretations of traditional Taoist practices as a means of improving the health of his students.

The society's long form and related exercises have a pronounced forward lean and emphasize large movements and stretching of the limbs and spine for health/energy purposes.

Wu

This style is a modification of the Yang family style of Yang Ban Hou, who was renowned for his bad temper and very martial approach to t'ai chi. The founder of Wu style, Wu Chian-chuan (1870–1942) reputedly adapted the Yang "small-circle" form to suit his own temperament and previous martial training.

The forms of this style have moderate postures and emphasize relatively small circular movements, powerful wrist rotations, and the use of fa-ching (discharging power). Wu continues to place more emphasis on martial function than most Yang styles as they exist today.

In addition to a slow form, this style has a fast form with swift and flexible movements. The most obvious characteristic of Wu style is its forward tilt in both form and the martial exercises. Wu is divided into "old" and "new" variations.

Sun

This style was created by Sun Lu-tang (1859–1933), a brilliant scholar and martial artist. It is the synthesis of his expertise in hsing-i, pa-kua, and a Yang style of t'ai chi. It contains the follow-up footwork of the first, the supple twisting of the second, and the continuous and circular movement of the third. This style is comparatively rare, even in China.

New Taijiquan

In the mid-1950s, the Communist Chinese government decided to standardize and popularize the practice of t'ai chi ch'uan to make it more accessible to the masses. The intent was also to de-emphasize the mystical and martial aspects of the art.

The resulting 24 and 88 posture sequences were based on the Yang style, while the 48 and 66 posture sequences were choreographed to combine the main techniques of all the major styles. The resulting forms of "new taijiquan" did prove easier to teach, and their daily use became widespread in China and eventually spread around the world.

However, they were also—quietly at first—decried by the traditionalists as being "watered-down" t'ai chi. Traditionalists felt that the forms had been incompetently redesigned for political reasons and were seriously flawed. The detractors of the new taiji, many of whom were trained in traditional Chinese medicine, argued that studying these forms was not only a waste of time from a martial point of view but that practicing them could affect the health adversely. This was due, they felt, to the way in which the forms had been rearranged with certain postures or their repetitions deleted or added without sufficient thought being given to how it would affect the internal movement of ch'i.

In recent years, perhaps as a partial admission that there was some truth to the charges, the Chinese government has begun to give limited support to preserving and spreading the traditional forms and martial exercises. However, the new taiji forms continue to serve the health and sport competition needs of the masses.

Finally, it is important to remember that those who have been loudest in their complaints about the government-sanctioned forms may well be wrong to a greater or lesser degree. By their very nature, traditionalists will resist change in their fields of expertise.

CHOOSING AN INSTRUCTOR

T'ai chi is an experiential process composed not only of its outward *form*, the postures and tactics unique to it, but to its *intent*, the creation, movement, and expression of energy. True familiarity with and understanding of such a process comes only through the intimacy of a give-and-take relationship, an informal apprenticeship, between instructor and student.

You must have or have had a teacher who is also determined to keep learning and is not simply content to pass on dead knowledge which may no longer fit into the scheme of things or which only is valid within the narrow universe of his/her influence.

Some would argue that a few exceptional individuals have

produced concepts so perfect that altering them would only debase their usefulness, and this may be true. If so, then whatever changes are made will, in the course of time, be revealed as flawed and, hopefully, the individuals making those changes will have learned from their failure to improve what already worked.

In the "good old days," if your martial art worked only in theory or in isolation, you frequently found out the hard way. It is still true in some countries or Chinese areas that someone opening a school will initially get a visit from established instructors who want immediate and pragmatic proof that the newcomer is qualified to teach. This isn't as true as it once was, and, as t'ai chi is a growth industry, many unqualified people (and a few charlatans or psychotics) are teaching what they consider to be t'ai chi and its related disciplines (health, self-defense, ch'i-kung).

The experienced practitioner or legitimate instructor can quickly see or feel just how skilled someone is at doing, if not teaching, t'ai chi. It is not so easy for the average beginner or intermediate student. What should you look for when searching for competent instruction?

Guidelines

Pay a visit to each school in your area and observe at least one class before making your choice. Especially in traditional schools, it is important to respect certain rules of etiquette when visiting for the first time:

• Watch at least one complete session and refrain from commenting on anything you see unless asked—and then be diplomatic.

• Never talk about how much you already know (it may be less than you think!), as this may be interpreted as a challenge.

• Never touch any weapons on display unless you request permission.

• Depreciate your own skills if asked but be ready to demonstrate if asked to do so politely.

• Smile and keep in mind how you would want a visitor to behave if he or she were visiting one of your classes.

In general, someone who teaches on a full-time basis (a professional) should have more skill/insights than someone who teaches part-time (an amateur). However, life is rarely so clear-cut, and it can be quite difficult to determine the level of an instructor's skills until you have actually been exposed to them (or their absence) for some time.

Don't be put off initially if an instructor teaches in his home or in a park. Having a large commercial school is not necessarily a sign that the instructor is worth studying with. It can be very difficult to transmit many of the concepts and skills of the art to large numbers of students.

Why work hard and pay well to be part of a large group being taught by other students who may only be teaching because the instructor can get their services for free or at low cost?

Conversely, just because an instructor teaches on a private or semiprivate basis doesn't necessarily mean that he is more noble or less concerned with profit. Sometimes, such instructors charge exorbitant rates, teach little of value, and use the one-on-one basis of their relationship to manipulate and exploit their students.

Ask for the instructor's background in whatever he or she is teaching, and do some research into the legitimacy of the style and any affiliations with national or international organizations. Avoid accepting as valid any vague claims to grand titles such as professor, grand master, founder, and sole instructor of a new system or style. It's a sad reflection on our times that the martial arts magazines are full of ads from organizations that will send you an impressive certificate of grading or membership for little or nothing beyond the fee they charge for such services.

The study of t'ai chi often went hand in hand with a knowledge of traditional Chinese medicine in "the old days." This is still true for a few teachers, but it is also important to remember that the title of "Dr." in front of a name can easily mean only that he or she has a Ph.D. in a field that has little relevance to t'ai chi.

Shun individuals (and they do exist) who claim to have learned from a secret society or in some untraceable monastery in the Far East—especially if they are not Oriental. Even worse is the individual who claims to be the reincarnation of a famous martial arts figure.

How do the students relate to the instructor and his or her senior students? Is the class atmosphere overly aggressive and competitive, or is it too relaxed, with more emphasis placed on drinking tea and discussing, rather than practicing, t'ai chi? You can tell a lot about an instructor by the type of people he or she attracts and retains as students.

A good instructor should be able to motivate and lead students to attain and, in some cases, surpass his or her own levels of ability. If none of an instructor's students seem to approach his level, it is probably because that instructor (consciously or subconsciously) surrounds himself with incompetent students, cannot tolerate those who train long enough to acquire skills that rival his own, or withholds "secrets" in order to maintain an edge over the pupils.

Does the instructor have a sense of humor, a family, and other interests that bring outside meaning to his life? You can learn many things from a humorless, obsessive, and single-minded instructor, but you may end up becoming more like him than you want. To a greater or lesser extent, we gradually mirror the characteristics of those whom we admire.

Be skeptical of grandiose accounts you may be given of an instructor's feats and abilities. Be wary also of out-of-condition instructors whose greatness may be in the past—if it ever existed. While you don't need to be slim to be healthy or able to defend yourself using t'ai chi principles and tactics, gross lack of conditioning should be a sign that self-discipline is not one of the instructor's strengths and probably won't be part of the curriculum.

In this regard, beware of those instructors who tell you that an enormous belly is a sign that they are full of ch'i. They may well be full of something, but it's more likely to be body fat! Conversely, be suspicious of instructors who are obviously into weight training and have bulging chest and arm muscles. There's nothing wrong with fitness, but such development should not be overemphasized. However, having just said that, in all fairness, the physical exercise of high-caliber t'ai chi work does tend to build up the muscle and sinews of the waist/lower body so that advanced practitioners are quite often thick through the trunk and upper legs.

Is there a balanced curriculum offered that will allow you to study those aspects of t'ai chi which most interest you? An instructor does not have to be proficient in the martial arts side of t'ai chi to teach form or related exercises for health purposes. However, my own prejudice leads me to believe that, given the choice, you should always select an instructor who understands t'ai chi as a martial art, even if you only want to learn form for health.

In terms of the martial side of the art, the instruction should neither be a study of streetfighting nor simply techniques executed against rigid attacks from a stationary position or with little movement or footwork. While full-contact training may be beyond your capabilities and is not necessary for learning basic self-defense skills, there should be an element of contact allowed so that you learn to deal with pain as well as how to avoid and inflict it. Controlled contact with a variety of partners using safety equipment is essential for developing realistic self-defense capabilities.

Beware of instructors who more or less guarantee progress in a certain amount of time. Fast learners do not always stay that way past a certain point, and slow starters may, by perseverance, become proficient. Size, sex, and age are not necessarily limiting factors to progress but realistically must be taken into account in terms of choosing the instructor who suits your needs.

In recent years, some schools/systems have adopted colored sash grading systems to motivate students. In some ways this is unnecessary, as a true internal martial artist is more concerned with inner growth than external progress. However, in physical terms, self-defense skills can only be built if you measure yourself against your peers. Consequently, a student of martial t'ai chi should measure his/her combat skill advancement against others in the class and against other more advanced students who, in turn, measure themselves against the instructor.

Finally, look for an instructor who will allow you to pay on a monthly or semimonthly basis; you may find that your interest or responsibilities change suddenly, and long-term contracts usually only benefit the school.

Beware of those instructors who insist on long-term contracts or large initial cash payments. By comparing rates at a variety of t'ai chi clubs, martial art dojos, or fitness facilities, you can determine what a fair monthly rate is in your area. While it is true that you generally have to pay for quality, it does not necessarily follow that the more expensive the instruction the higher the quality. North Americans are used to judging a product by its cost and are likely to assume that something free or relatively inexpensive is probably inferior.

THE INSTRUCTOR: COACH OR TEACHER?

The *Concise Oxford English Dictionary* defines a teacher as someone who instructs a skill or academic course and a coach as someone who trains a pupil intensively or individually.

As with anyone who transmits a worthwhile skill and/or understanding, the t'ai chi instructor must be both a coach and teacher to his or her students. The difference between the two definitions may seem small, but it is crucial to the development of the student.

The beginning student needs to be taught the basics of stance, breathing, relaxation, proper movement, and a host of other characteristics that make t'ai chi different from other martial arts/healing activities.

At this level, the student is very much learning by attempting to copy the external movements of the instructor. Fairly large groups can be taught through this method, and the majority will learn at an adequate pace and to a certain basic level of proficiency. The more advanced student, however, will need to experience the "coach" side of his or her instructor to appreciate and develop the intuitive and subtle aspects of form practice and, especially, to learn interactive skills.

Unfortunately, it was very much the tradition (and still is in many schools) for the instructor to coach (i.e., work intensively and individually) with only one or two select students. This ensures secrecy if it is deemed valuable by the teacher, and it ensures that the real feel of t'ai chi is only transmitted to those he or she feels are worthy.

However, this also ensures that only a few people—usually those with natural talent—are likely to be exposed to the one-on-one coaching that creates the ideal environment for the maximum growth of a student's understanding of and skill in t'ai chi. This is not to deny that the senior students can, in turn, pass on what they've learned to the larger group. However, think of it this way: bottled spring water never has quite the same taste as that drunk at the source.

To be fair to the potential of as many t'ai chi players as possible, an instructor must learn to differentiate between the coaching and teaching side of transmitting t'ai chi and do what is appropriate for the needs of each of his or her students.

It is true that a one-on-one relationship is very demanding of the time, skill, and emotional energy of both instructor and student. Perhaps it is impossible to have this kind of apprenticeship relationship with more than one or two students at a time. However, it is not impossible for an instructor to limit the size of classes so that he or she gets the chance to work with each student, even if only for a few minutes, during class time. This is of particular importance to transmitting whatever competence he or she may have at push-hands and self-defense.

If you are just beginning to train in t'ai chi or are looking for an instructor, it may be wise to reconsider the individual who overemphasizes the "teaching" side of t'ai chi, preferring to lecture and demonstrate, or who only really works with one or two senior students.

As a novice, you will need to have an exceptional aptitude for t'ai chi to learn beyond a certain point of competency from such an individual.

Like the balancing act that is t'ai chi, balancing the two sides of instruction is essential if all students (the gifted, the average, and the untalented) are to be best served without compromising the needs of the instructor.

It is sad to say that for those searching for a "quick fix," t'ai chi is no different from any other worthwhile endeavor—to get results, one must invest time and effort. If you are in poor health or out of condition when you start, you just have that much more to overcome before you begin to see the real benefits of your training.

It is true that t'ai chi depends much less on physical effort, especially at advanced levels, than other, related disciplines. Even in terms of their self-defense skills, many of the experts I have met were in their prime, despite being in their forties and fifties.

However, it is equally true that, for the beginner and intermediate student, much more mental and physical effort are needed than is first apparent to the casual observer. Many beginners are shocked and discouraged that their first sessions leave them with stiff shoulders or sore legs.

The skills and attitudes of t'ai chi are often quite foreign to beginners, even those who are intellectually and physically active. In

CHAPTER 3

LEARNING
HOW TO
LEARN

many ways, learning how to learn t'ai chi is partly a process of shedding your preconceptions and misconceptions to allow yourself to benefit from your training.

For example, if you think that doing the slow form is the only legitimate expression of t'ai chi, you may well never even try any of the other approaches—fast forms or those which combine slow and fast movements. When you decide prematurely what is correct and what isn't, you severely limit your potential for growth. It's like trying to get my six-year-old son to eat liver. He knows he "hates it," even though the substance has never even touched his lips!

Learning to observe what you are seeing demonstrated is the first and, in some ways, the hardest lesson. In China, t'ai chi form was traditionally taught almost without dialogue, and questions were discouraged—often harshly. For those few who wanted to learn the martial tactics, learning was through the hard-knocks method: endless drilling in the basics and working with more experienced students who used you as a dummy.

If you persevered, despite being battered about or repeatedly thrown into the wall, you caught on to the proper methods—sooner or later. The teacher led the class or observed, and everyone followed along as best they could while trying to copy the movements of the teacher or the more experienced students.

When Chinese instructors began teaching larger numbers of Westerners, this teaching method was hindered by the language barrier, as most spoke little or poor English. Those who taught the martial methods of the art continued to teach the way they had been taught or gave up teaching these aspects because North Americans were unable, or unwilling, to train so strongly.

Unfortunately, many Western instructors teach this way as well because they are automatically copying the methods used to teach them. North Americans are not used to such an approach and can find it difficult to cope with—and rightly so. By contrast, the use of progressive escalation of training intensity and verbal coaching eases the learning process considerably, as long as it's not overdone.

Sadly, it is true that talking about t'ai chi often overshadows practicing its various aspects in many schools. While it is essential to discuss its principles and to study its theoretical and historical side, true understanding only comes from *effort*.

Really observing what the instructor is doing takes a great deal of attentiveness and is, in some ways, impossible for those who do not know what to look for. It is only when you are technically comfortable with the external movements of the form and various exercises that you can begin to internalize your understanding of them.

It is only at this level (which can take months or years to reach) that you can learn how to see the wealth of details and subtle movements that are needed to make substantial progress.

Even on a superficial level, being attentive in this way requires that you watch your role model several times before attempting to copy his or her movements. Many students try to copy as they observe, and the ambitious may also try to watch the others around them or themselves in any available mirrors all at the same time.

Having learned to watch the actions and attributes that you need to copy, the next step is trying to repeat the movements for yourself. Once you have become competent at copying, at some point in your t'ai chi career you will begin to be a little more creative in terms of putting more of yourself into your practice instead of just trying to mimic your instructor.

With perseverance, hard work, and a little aptitude at some point in your t'ai chi evolution, you will begin to truly digest the principles of the art and make them your own. To achieve a real feel for the art, you must learn to "be" the movement and not "do" the movement.

However, it is also true that the more you learn, the easier it will become to learn even more material. I have seen expert instructors repeat forms that they had just seen demonstrated for the first time. While such skills belong to the exceptional (and even they don't perform the forms flawlessly after one viewing), it is inspirational.

On a more mundane level, it has been my experience, and that of others I have trained or worked with, that it does become much easier to learn new material once you have internalized the principles common to a style. For most of us, such an evolution is the work of many years and is a process which can be short-circuited at many points in our training. In addition, such learning skills also have their own potential dangers if the mind's ability to learn outpaces the physical capabilities of the one learning.

For example, one of my students—a talented instructor in her own right—taught herself a new long form from a video in just over three weeks. Her experience and intuition eased the learning process; however, she could not adjust so quickly to practicing a form which used slightly different muscles and patterns of movement from those her body was used to. As a result, she suffered a severe lower-back injury from forcing her body to match her mental comprehension.

Learning can be a very frustrating process for those of us not gifted with any particular innate talent for the discipline being learned. However, having a natural aptitude can also have its downside in that rapid initial progress can lead to emotional smugness on the part of the practitioner.

The art is meant to last a lifetime in the sense that it can be enjoyed and practiced with benefit by anyone who practices regularly, consistently, and moderately. It cannot be learned quickly, especially if studied as a martial art, but the skills and attitudes can be cumulative. That which is gained does not fade in the same way that strength and stamina do with increasing age.

Consequently, the importance of *becoming* is somewhat diminished. If you concentrate on becoming, you will find that you easily lose heart with the value of your practice if you do not make the progress you would like or if it seems inferior to that of your classmates.

Conversely, while training in t'ai chi can last years, it is not enough to say that *being* is more important than becoming. Those superficially content with "going with the flow" or "being laid back" are not likely to engage in enough effort to begin understanding the real lessons of t'ai chi. For the beginner to intermediate student, the greatest requirement for absorbing the art is the initial tedium of repetition!

Those who are obsessive perfectionists and realize that t'ai chi might fill some needs in their life are, in some ways, more likely to gain some skill at the art than those beginners who are already "mellow." The former are, at least, driven to practice on a regular basis because of their personality, while the latter practice—or don't—as the whim takes them.

Taoism, as a philosophy, is largely about establishing a sense of balance and proportion in life or any aspect of it. If you are completely without a desire to become, the danger exists that you will become listless in your attitudes and practice and that you will be content to play at being aimless in the sense of not caring what happens in terms of your training and life. This is most likely to happen in those schools of t'ai chi which neglect or dilute push-hands and combat skills. But it is difficult to remain inattentive when someone is willing to take advantage of it by flinging you across the room or painfully locking your elbow!

After demonstrating a technique which had left me vulnerable, one of my former instructors used to say, "Sometimes, it is good to feel the power." He wasn't exercising a sadistic streak in using that power judiciously, as I was never really hurt by his tactics. It was his way of forcing me to pay attention immediately.

Conversely, too much fighting or "feeling the power" may discourage some from continuing their training or sharpen the reactions and attitudes of others to the point of paranoia. Again, it's a question of balance, isn't it?

THE NECESSARY LEARNING TOOLS

Keeping that balance in mind, here is the great secret of t'ai chi—there is none! Long-term, moderate effort under the supervision of a competent instructor will, eventually, lead you to realize skills and the value of the art in a way that analysis and logic never can.

If you feel somehow cheated by such a suggestion, I would suggest that you examine your intellectual or emotional need to be part of a mysterious process. The Taoist classics suggest that the most complex results can spring from an understanding of the simple. Yet those who are attracted to the art because it can seem miraculous and because it has the exotic appeal of coming from a culture rich in wisdom and age compared to our own can easily fall into the trap of demanding complexity when none is needed.

The need to know, to feel that you are sharing something

unique, is invariably tied to the psychological need to feel that what you are learning is somehow the only true way and that "lesser" students are practicing false or less important ways. However, in life as in t'ai chi, the simplest answers are often the most sage, and it is too easy to miss the forest because one is concentrating on the trees.

All too often, people seem unable to accept anything as valid unless it has complicated theories which satisfy the intellect's need to overanalyze. Such analysis *can* lead to wisdom. Unfortunately, the Western tendency for overanalysis often leads instead to greater confusion.

Those with a natural aptitude for the art will learn more quickly and achieve greater results than the less gifted, but that is a sad truth in life. We are not created equal in all ways. However, *anyone* can learn t'ai chi and benefit from its practice.

The benefits, the personal growth to be derived from t'ai chi practice, depend on several emotional factors:

Desire

Wanting to learn and to be as good as (or better than) your instructor is both counterproductive and essential, depending on your motives and level of maturity.

If you, as a student, don't want to improve, you won't—in effect, self-hypnotizing yourself into failing to ever really achieve your potential. Similarly, if you don't think that you can eventually equal or surpass your instructor's abilities, then you won't.

Effort

To make progress in any art, hard work and discipline are necessary. However, you must be careful that you don't become too serious or obsessive about it. You must train regularly in its various practices and skills, but without becoming so obsessive that you are injured or become imbalanced in the other aspects of your life.

In other words, you must allow yourself to practice for the fun of it and not just because you think t'ai chi is some form of miraculous Oriental package that will fill all of your needs.

Faith

You must have (or develop) the faith in yourself that allows you to continue to train even after those sessions that leave you depressed about your ability to learn and make progress. You can suffer such temporary losses of self-confidence at any point in your t'ai chi career, and they are just part of the price you must pay for growing as a practitioner or instructor.

An injured ego is like a superficial bruise on the body—it hurts at first, but you can't do much about it. The pain and discoloration will fade with time, and you won't even remember where the bruise was in the future. For more damaging emotional and physical bruises, you can't ignore the hurt but should re-examine the cause so you can take steps to ensure that the injury is not repeated.

You must also have faith in your instructor without being blind to his or her failings. The lifelong process of learning t'ai chi demands the guidance and instruction of someone who knows and loves the art. However, it is also true that few of us are willing to admit that we are unable to learn because there is something wrong with whatever we are being taught—lack of faith in yourself is as damaging to progress as too much faith.

It is important to trust your intuition so that if you are trying to learn a style or a system that is not right for you or that is in itself flawed, you can admit that.

Humility

You must be willing to "empty your teacup" even as you fill it again and again so that you never reach that miserable level of egotism in which you believe that you've learned everything there is to know. You must be humble, even if you've made considerable progress. Most approaches to t'ai chi have some merit and can teach some valuable lesson, even if those lessons only fulfill the narrow needs of the moment.

If you can maintain a sense of perspective on your understanding of the art, then you will continue to make progress. Don't let arrogance underwrite your inability to make progress past a certain point.

Love

You must be like a child in terms of the all-embracing nature and ease with which children will embrace a beloved object or person.

In other words, you have to love the art to make progress beyond mere technical understanding. This emotion is mystical only in the sense that it brings a sense of deep fulfillment. This comes not from selfishness, fear, or wanting to excel at the art, but from the love of doing the activity for its own sake.

However, loving t'ai chi, like loving God, yourself, your fellow man, or any endeavor, does not imply that you will automatically be better than someone who doesn't. Some sources and teachers would like us to believe otherwise, but I feel that this is because they were never tested by anyone outside their own narrow universe.

Loving t'ai chi guarantees only that your life will be enriched by the exercise and health aspects as well as what you learn about yourself and how you react to life.

Patience

You must have or develop patience so that, to paraphrase Chen Wei-ming, (one of Yang Chen-fu's senior disciples and a famous instructor in his own right), if in ten years you don't succeed, you use twenty!

Frustration comes from within; it is not something imposed by the difficulty of learning any art or discipline. While the stimuli for frustration comes from poor performance, how you relate to that poor performance is uniquely a function of your personality.

Like anything else, frustration with your progress can be a two-edged sword. If not frustrated to a certain point, the student is likely to be complacent in his or her training. If overly frustrated, the student is likely to give up prematurely. This happens when the student feels, rightly or wrongly, that there is something wrong with him if he cannot learn at all or even simply quickly enough for his own taste.

Frustration comes because you expect too much too soon and because, paradoxically, you work too hard (especially mentally) when training. If you can learn to pace yourself in your efforts, progress will come eventually. And it is not just a matter of nodding your head in agreement and saying, "Yes, that's right." You have to believe it on a gut level.

Self-Knowledge

T'ai chi should not be something you do because you want to be good at it, nor a superficial veneer that you assume for a few hours every week like some T-shirt with a fancy logo. It is simply another name for seeing yourself, your environment, and the interrelationship of the two with greater clarity.

If "I" do not know how "I" feel about t'ai chi, then the art remains something outside of me that is observed instead of digested.

A Zen (the Japanese version of Chinese Ch'an Buddhism, which was a fusion of Indian Buddhist with Taoist thought) monk was asked if the Buddha nature was in everything, even in dung! He said yes.

The Buddha nature (the Tao) is found in those who have digested something so that its substance becomes part of them. Seen this way, human by-products, whether dung or t'ai chi skills, are part of the ongoing process of understanding your own nature and the nature of existence.

Being aware of yourself and your environment and how they interact are central to the study of t'ai chi as a means of psychological and spiritual enlightenment. It is also central to self-defense: if I cannot recognize the danger in a situation or opponent, I cannot react to it; if I cannot respond swiftly and intuitively to a variety of attacks, I cannot hope to survive.

There is another Zen parable about a scholar who was bragging to a monk about his great spiritual powers. The monk listened politely and then asked the braggart what he had noticed in the foyer when coming into the building. The scholar was unable to recall anything he'd seen but dismissed that as unimportant. The monk smiled and suggested that awareness which did not extend to the mundane was perhaps not as sublime as claimed.

Self-knowledge is not a a blind introspection but an exploration of yourself in relation to your environment and those you interact with. This is nowhere truer than when doing t'ai chi: you must be totally aware of how and why you are moving while being paradoxically uninvolved with the process. This is as true when doing form as when working with a partner.

THE VALUE OF SEMINARS
FOR CONTINUING GROWTH

Since I began teaching in 1985 and stopped training regularly with my main instructor, Allan Weiss, I have tried to attend at least one weekend seminar per year with a more "mature" instructor than myself. Except for absolute beginners, who may just be confused by material unlike that which they are trying to learn, everyone can benefit from exposure to such seminars.

No matter what the level of skill or experience, few experienced students or "junior" instructors are so well-balanced that they can't benefit either from experiencing a different (possibly superior) "feel" for t'ai chi or a different physical expression of it. In fact, *balancing* the proportions of our internal/external (function/form) understanding of t'ai chi is the real benefit of attending such seminars.

Relative beginners get the opportunity to sample the wares of advanced practitioners, which will help them decide what directions their training needs to take; intermediate students get to experience approaches to the art that may be very different from what they're used to; and advanced practitioners get to talk and train with others in a setting that encourages them to learn (and not compete on a physical or psychological level) from each other.

Such workshops can help overcome the tendency of practitioners and instructors alike to reach a plateau in their development and remain fixated there. Such plateaus can be due to inadequate or improper training or to misplaced loyalty to a former instructor who feels that his or her interpretation of t'ai chi is the best.

How many of us have refused to attend such workshops because we felt it would be disrespectful to our current instructor? I have in the past, and I don't think I'm alone in that regard. While it is important to respect your own teachers and styles, it is also important to try to see t'ai chi, even if only for a moment, from as many perspectives as possible.

Even worse, if you deny yourself the opportunity to train with a variety of talented people simply because you are overly confident of your skills or because you fear being compared to others, you lose the opportunity to grow as a practitioner.

This is perhaps of greater importance if you are instructing; you do your own students a great disservice by failing to get those insights that might help you to help them develop. In addition, your rigid example may make them reluctant to explore the workshop learning process for themselves.

Such seminars do help us "old dogs" remember how to learn new tricks. During a university project in the United States a few years ago, researchers discovered that you could teach an old dog new tricks as long as it had never got out of the habit of learning. In other words, if an animal hadn't had to learn anything since it was young, it had a great deal of difficulty relearning the learning process.

Sadly for t'ai chi practitioners, this also seems true of humans. If we get out of the habit of learning, it becomes very difficult to relearn the skills necessary for the learning process.

Often, the real challenge in training at such seminars lies in not succumbing to despair when comparing one's own lesser abilities to those teaching. It becomes essential to see such instructors as sources of inspiration to our own efforts rather than as sources of discouragement or envy.

We are fortunate in North America that many extremely talented instructors are available through short-term workshops. No matter what your style, skill, or experience, a few hours or perhaps days of applying yourself with more experienced instructors can bring results that would take months or years (or possibly never come) if you were working on your own or solely with the instructor(s) of your own style.

One of the marvels of t'ai chi is that no matter how deeply you go into it, there are always new things to learn. If, for example, William C.C. Chen, Dr. Yang Jwing-Ming, Master Liang Shou-yu, and Sam Masich can value their mutual exchange of ideas, it would be presumptuous for the rest of us to assume that we can learn nothing new about t'ai chi.

The foundation of this art is the long-term practice of a solo sequence. On a basic level, the practice of such forms involves memorizing and repeating a series of linked postures created as a way of improving health and internal energy flow and practicing self-defense tactics without a partner.

Unlike the choreographed sequences in the external martial arts, t'ai chi form, as it has evolved—particularly in the Yang style—is as concerned with improving the overall health of the practitioner as it is with those aspects useful for combat (speed, strength, and cardiovascular fitness).

Long-term repetition of these patterns eventually leads to an intuitive understanding of the interaction of mental and physical effort. In this way, the practitioner learns to be holistically balanced and energetic. Traditionally trained instructors and the medical researchers of mainland China believe that the proper practice of form can create and maintain good health. In the Orient, the art is routinely prescribed

CHAPTER 4

SOLO FORM: THE FOUNDATION OF T'AI CHI

by doctors as an *adjunct* therapy for conditions that run the gamut from high blood pressure and arthritis to emotional problems. However, its main role is in the prevention of many ailments.

Many of the disorders best treated with its practice are those which can be psychosomatic in origin. However, it is important to remember that a psychosomatic disorder causes real pain and physical symptoms. The origin of the malaise may be the mind and the emotions rather than the body, but the suffering is far from imaginary. Curing such disorders is no less essential than curing those caused by injury or infection.

Whether the benefits of form practice come through "faith healing" or "positive thinking" or because of the validity of t'ai chi's theoretical basis is impossible to determine—and largely immaterial to the potential results.

Each practitioner will experience benefits depending on his or her faith, the expertise of the instructor, and the amount and quality of practice.

LAYING A FOUNDATION

Think of t'ai chi form practice as being like creating the foundation for a home: understanding the principles allows you to dig a hole—a defined emptiness; competence at the individual postures (whatever the style) provides the building blocks; and the creation of a beneficial flow of energy is the cement that binds the blocks into a strong structure.

The "Rules" of Form

The following rules apply, in detail, to the Yang style I follow and may contradict some of what you have been told by your own instructor. When in doubt, ask the instructor why he or she does such-and-such. A good instructor will be able to explain why he or she follows a particular interpretation, and not just by saying, "That's how I learned it!"

The rules of form are interpreted differently by different instructors—even within the same style—for the most part without prejudice to their students.

◆ Energy is rooted and generated in the lower limbs, directed by the waist, transmitted through the spine, and expressed by the upper limbs. Use only the necessary muscular effort to flow from one posture to another, neither too tense nor too limp.

◆ Form practice is a state of *awareness*, not of partial or total introspection. You must simultaneously pay attention to each of the following: yourself and your environment, your mind and your body, your torso and your legs, your right and your left hand, etc.

◆ Breathe in while moving the arms toward the body and expanding the abdominal area. Breathe out while moving the arms away from the body and contracting the abdominal area. (N.B., Many instructors recommend that you do the exact opposite of this, in particular when developing certain martial skills.) In general, you should match one full breath (in and out) with each posture in form. With time, you will learn to slow down your rate of respiration and, in this way, slow down your physical movement.

◆ Except for moments of transition, the weight is never distributed equally onto both legs. This is called being "double-weighted" and is considered one of the worst errors in t'ai chi. Depending on the style and instructor, 70 to 90 percent of your weight should be on one leg when you complete a posture.

◆ One foot should never be directly in front of the other. The recommended width and depth of stance vary from style to style.

◆ Always "scout ahead" with your leg/foot when stepping forward. Land on the heel and drop forward onto the foot *slowly* as you shift forward. When stepping back, "scout behind" with the foot, landing on the ball and shifting *slowly* to the heel.

◆ The weight-supporting knee should be aligned with the toes of the foot on that leg. Never allow it to sag inward due to inattention or overbending, as such misalignment strains the ligaments of the knee joint.

◆ The ankle must be relaxed and express the concept of yin and yang in terms of the relevant positions of the heel and ball of the foot for each posture.

◆ The abdomen/tan tien/torso must move the limbs through three dimensions: turning/twisting to either side, shifting forward or back, and stretching up or down.

◆ The tailbone (coccyx) must be "tucked under" at all times. This means that your pelvis is tilted and your buttocks relaxed.

◆ All joints in the body must "open and close" to facilitate movement on a physical and internal level. In some cases (e.g., spine, hips), the actual physical movement is quite small, but it's essential and best learned under the supervision of an experienced instructor.

◆ The shoulders are never shrugged or tense, but rather rounded and relaxed. This should not be confused with having stiff, hunched shoulders like those of a bad Western boxer.

◆ The elbows are never locked, but are flexible at all times.

◆ The wrists must express the concept of yin and yang in coordination with the movement of each posture (i.e., be bent or straight as necessary).

◆ In general, it is preferable to lean *slightly* forward when doing postures rather than confusing straightness with a rigid spine, which is often accompanied by a slight backward lean.

◆ The head is held as if suspended at the crown, without any slack in the connecting material from the ceiling. The head feels comfortable only if held "just so." In this way, your lower half feels strongly rooted while your upper half feels supple and stretched gently upward.

◆ The mouth should be closed, the tongue held lightly against the palate. This serves two purposes: it completes the visualization of a closed circuit of the breath/ch'i from the base of the torso to the crown of the head, and it helps keep the tongue away from the teeth (in case your jaws are struck and you inadvertently bite yourself).

◆ You should return to your starting point when you finish a form, partly because doing so is excellent exercise in terms of maintaining the proper stances/stepping and partly because it symbolizes your return to a state of "central equilibrium" (wu chi).

◆ Even though the form and its component postures look as if they are composed of straight lines, all movements have an overt or subtle circularity.

◆ You should practice long form at least once a day to get any health benefits and three times per day to gain any real skill. On a simplistic level, the repetitions should be one after the other: the first serving as a warm-up, the second as the true exercise, and the third as a cool-down.

In general, the longer it takes you to do form, the better! One of the few areas of agreement among the majority of modern experts is that long form should take a minimum of twenty minutes to complete, and the slower the better—as long as the form does not degenerate into a random stop-and-go process. However, this is valid only for slow forms, as there are also slow/fast and fast forms of various lengths. Not surprisingly, there is controversy over whether or not you should ever do the slow forms quickly as a martial exercise. Some authorities say this should never be done, that your fast training should be with other routines. Conversely, some say that you should practice a slow form quickly—once you can do it properly at a slow pace.

In terms of effort, sweating is also a controversial issue. Some authorities feel that excessive sweating is good, as it means you are flushing toxins out of your system. Others feel that excessive sweating is a sign that your yin and yang energies are not properly balanced and you are working too hard physically. A little common sense is essential, especially if you are training outside on a hot day. After all, sweating is the body's main means of maintaining body temperature.

Rooting: Using the Lower Body

You should feel as if your soles are sinking into whatever surface you are standing upon—as when making footprints in wet sand. It is essential to do this, as just thinking about the soles of the feet resting on the surface of the ground does not improve the quality of your rooting as dramatically.

Being rooted should not be confused with being immobile, although it often is. While you feel as if you are sunk into the surface you stand on, you must also be able to move freely as necessary. With time, you learn to step firmly but lightly, like a cat stalking a mouse.

The notion of drawing energy from the earth is not unique to the Orient. Even Westerners talk about "keeping your feet firmly on the ground," in reference to having a realistic approach to life.

When reduced to its most basic physical level, keeping the knees bent (the angle depending on the form and the preference of the instructor) allows the legs to have the give which is necessary to safely support the body and provide a springy potential for movement. A stiff, overly straight leg is more likely to be injured if forced to bear a greater weight than normal. Keeping the knees bent also gives those joints room to absorb punishment through speedy movement if suddenly kicked or struck.

Stances that are extremely low, narrow, or wide are frequently advocated, especially by traditional instructors. These can be beneficial in terms of improving muscular strength and joint flexibility. However, such stances do not allow for ease of movement. Stances that are overly narrow allow speed but tend to impede balance, the turning of the waist, and stability.

There remains a wide variety of interpretations of how narrow or wide the stance should be, even among the instructors of a particular style, and this can be quite confusing for beginners. My own opinion is that the feet should remain roughly shoulder-width apart and the knees moderately flexed. This stance allows stability without compromising the ability to move quickly while remaining balanced.

Centering: The Use of the Waist

To quote one of the t'ai chi classics, "The source of the postures lies in the waist."

The waist and the physical part of the body referred to as the lower tan tien (the ball visualized between the crotch and the navel) becomes, with time, effort, and correct coaching, the main pivot for the body and the origin of movement for the limbs.

Such movement of the waist/torso has three dimensions: turning/spiraling from side to side, shifting forward and back, and stretching up and down. Of the three, up and down and turning/spiraling are the most difficult to perform correctly. The former is not just a coarse bobbing movement and must be effectively synchronized with the latter as a gentle twisting of the spinal column. The actual physical movement in both cases, while crucial, is relatively small.

I have used the following analogies in describing the three-dimensional movement of the body's center with some success in terms of helping my students to visualize the use of the lower tan tien on a physical level.

You can think of the abdomen as being like a gyroscope, which is usually a wheel mounted in a frame so that it can spin about an axis in any direction. A whirling gyroscope will resist changes in the orientation of its spin axis and is used in guidance systems and in toys (like t'ai chi, it has its serious and its playful implications).

When spinning, a gyroscope seems in some ways to be motionless but is really turning smoothly and quickly. Similarly, when doing t'ai chi, your physical center (leaving ch'i theories aside for the moment) should be imagined to be like a gyroscope, turning smoothly, balanced in all aspects of its movement.

When you hit a whirling gyroscope, it will bounce off and continue as if nothing had happened. This can be likened to the "bounce energy" that some t'ai chi players have in push-hands. However, if the axis of the gyroscope is affected, it (or a t'ai chi player) will begin to wobble and eventually fall. Similarly, if the speed of the gyroscope is not even and drops below a certain point it will begin to wobble, imperceptibly at first, and is more likely to be affected adversely if struck.

So a practitioner must keep his gyroscope's axis (the spine) centered and must turn the ball shape in the tan tien smoothly, not erratically, when doing form or trying to generate or repel force.

You can also imagine the movement of the waist and the body to be like a set of gears meshed together. You can think of the waist as the master gear; the shoulders, elbows, and wrists (or the joints of the legs) as subsidiary gears; and the mind as the impulse that starts and stops the interaction of the gears.

Some gears are large (the waist) and some small (the wrists), but the energy provided by their synchronized movement is much greater than that which could be provided by any of the component gears if they were turning on their own. In addition, some of the gears seem to move much faster or much slower than others (depending on their relative sizes), but all are moving as one because of their interdependence. If you start or stop one gear, you start or stop them all.

Similarly, the t'ai chi player in motion may seem to be moving his limbs at slightly different speeds, but all movement is really connected to the waist.

This has not been an attempt to reduce t'ai chi to a mechanistic level or deny that ch'i exists and is a factor in the energy development/movement process. Describing the lower tan tien in such terms is simply a way of making its movement more easily imagined by the average student.

INTERNAL EXERCISE:
THE ROLE OF THE TORSO

After the common cold, problems with the spine are among the most common medical concerns in North America. Such problems, especially in the lower back, were less common a century ago, partly because people didn't live long enough for the spine to deteriorate as part of the aging process. In addition, people were much more physically active; our increasingly sedentary life-styles have contributed to the magnitude of the problem.

In addition, human beings are poorly designed for being upright. Being able to stand and see farther while using two front feet to manipulate tools has many advantages, as our primate ancestors discovered. However, despite genetic adaptation over the millennia, using the spine to support weight in a vertical, rather than horizontal, manner is partly the cause for the frequency of back pain. An explanation of the construction of the spine will lend some understanding to why it so often lets us down when abused.

The twenty-four vertebrae that make up this flexible column are divided into three groups which, as a unit, form a gentle double-S curve to help absorb physical stress. In fact, the spine, far from being ramrod straight (contrary to what the military and some t'ai chi instructors would have us believe), is designed to curve so as to create a shock-absorber effect against sudden shock to maintain both its own integrity and that of the brain.

Each vertebra has two parts: the drumlike anterior section

closest to the front of the body attached to a bony antlerlike projection which encases the spinal cord. The vertebrae are stacked one on top of the other and are separated by twenty-three flexible discs. Like tires, these discs can change shape and return to their original donut shape after being deformed by sudden outside pressure or to facilitate movement.

During the day, under pressure of gravity, discs are slowly compressed so that we actually shrink. At night, they absorb water and nutrients and we wake a little taller than when we went to bed.

As we get older, these discs lose some of their ability to retain water and become less flexible—and so do we. In addition, as the discs harden and shrink with increasing age we lose some of the height we had in our physical prime.

Ligaments bind vertebrae and discs together, helping to support the spine while preventing us from making excessive movements in any direction. Short and long muscles (especially those in the abdomen) allow us to move while bracing the spine like the guy-wires on a tower antenna.

Few problems can frustrate patient and doctor as much as lower-back pain. Such pain can be slow to resolve and apt to recur. The sufferer's frustration and sense of helplessness then becomes part of a vicious cycle: injury causes muscle spasm, spasm induces pain, and the pain results in additional muscle spasm.

Though such involuntary muscular rigidity is intended by nature to immobilize the traumatized part temporarily, prolonged tension can increase the problem rather than help it. Learning and practicing form helps to relax and strengthen the soft tissues connected to the spine which, in turn, allows relaxed and efficient posture and movement.

Traditionally, the t'ai chi approach to spinal alignment is to encourage a posture that is childlike. However, if you observe toddlers who have mastered walking, you will notice that, while their posture is obviously centered and balanced, they lean forward slightly.

The photos of the famous Yang Chen-fu performing his form clearly show this modest forward lean in many of the postures. On the other hand, many instructors (even in the Yang style) either overemphasize this forward tilt or insist that the spine be too vertical.

An internal approach to the use of the spine during form (and eventually in daily life) would advocate that you learn to free it of unnecessary tension so that it becomes (and remains) a movable and flexible series of weight-supporting articulations—not a steel pipe!

Of equal importance to exercising the spine is exercising and strengthening the tendons, organs, and muscles of the torso. The different postures in the t'ai chi form are designed to benefit the internal organs and biological processes. For example, Single Whip is designed to strengthen the lungs, Wave Hands Like Clouds is used to alleviate mild hypertension (high blood pressure) and gastric ulcers, and Brush Knee and Push strengthens the lower digestive track.

Through long-term form practice, the spine and torso learn to compress and expand while simultaneously twisting gently in unison with the breathing. You learn to create energy waves with such movement, which are stored or transmitted as necessary.

Anyone who has experienced such "body breathing" will know how its experience revolutionizes your appreciation of form (and your ability to create wave as opposed to linear impact energy for martial purposes). However, like anything else, it is important not to become fixated on your ability to do this. It is just another step in that long process of self-understanding through t'ai chi.

SPIRIT: THE USE OF THE HEAD/MIND

Form teaches the importance of being attentive to the present (i.e., if you don't concentrate on physical details like turning the head in unison with the torso, then you lose some of your spiraling energy) and restores the natural sense of "awareness" that becomes deadened by the intellect's preoccupation with the need to control and analyze.

The practitioner begins form with stillness and returns to it at the end of the sequence. However, there is both a psychological and physical quiet within the movement of form—the former is constant, and the latter occurs at those almost imperceptible pauses at the end of each posture.

Many beginners are disappointed that they can't feel relaxed immediately when learning form. It's natural to want quick results, but it is important to remember that you can hardly relax physically when you are feeling mental stress as a result of the effort to get used to new principles of being.

In the beginning, practitioners are often so concerned with details that it is almost impossible to relax, and they may even feel more tense when they leave class than when they arrived. It is only as you grow comfortable with the physical details of form that you can relax enough to pay attention to the movement of your body and not just to details. It is that paying attention to the movement which helps create a relaxation that permeates the practitioner.

The amount of media exposure given to the subject of stress has helped many become aware of how it affects them. You can't correct a problem (especially when its symptoms are often vague) until you're aware of it. However, human nature being what it is, if you read enough negative material, you'll probably begin to feel that you, too, are affected—even if you were previously unaware of any such problems.

In a study of 106 healthy people in 1990, doctors at the University of Pittsburgh School of Medicine found that those in their study who had the most cold and flu infections also had the lowest number of "natural killer" (NK) cells in their immunological systems. These were the same subjects who had reported more intense and disruptive levels of stress in their lives. While the evidence wasn't conclusive, researchers felt that learning relaxation techniques to reduce ongoing stress would likely lead to an increase of NK cells and thus improve resistance to common viral infections.

Scare tactics by medical and social scientists and media overexposure aside, it should be obvious to even the most conservative that it makes sense to reduce ongoing stress levels. This is particularly important for those over thirty, as they are the ones most likely to develop medical conditions related to the physiological effects of long-term stress on the human body: heart disease, diminished immune-system response, and high blood pressure, among others.

Calming the mind releases some of the physical tension that

we accumulate in our bodies. Many people are overly analytical, and such therapies are ways of learning to see how absurdly active the mind can be and how easily we can become disassociated from our emotional and physical selves.

Recent Chinese studies have noted that the average participant experiences a reduction in blood pressure while doing form and for some time after concluding practice. However, by contrast, some North American medical evaluations of t'ai chi (Knowlton & Mucci, University of Southern Illinois, 1986; Zhou, Shephard, Plyley & Davis, University of Toronto, 1984) have shown that it may increase blood pressure slightly—if the style being practiced requires very low stances or if the student overexerts him or herself.

As in all matters of mental/physical health, the best method of dealing with stress is prevention. T'ai chi training will, in the long-run, improve the efficiency of the lungs so that you "relearn" how to breathe. Under stress, whether emotional or physical, many people tend to hold their breath or take shallow, rapid breaths. T'ai chi trains you to breathe deeply and efficiently.

Form also introduces the student to energy creation, flow, and discharge. The mind plays an essential role in producing any such benefits. To my understanding, there are two main camps of thought on this subject, both based on slightly different interpretations of a key passage in one of the t'ai chi classics. Both are valid interpretations, and the one you follow will depend on what you're looking for when you're doing form.

The first camp feels that flow must be uninterrupted for ch'i (energy) to circulate; the other camp feels that there should be a slight pause at the end of each posture (not each movement, each posture—many of the latter contain a number of movements (e.g., Grasp Bird's Tail to the Right contains ward-off, roll-back, etc.). It is felt that such pauses are necessary to practice the discharge of energy.

The "pause" method can give a better understanding of energy discharge, especially for beginners. For meditation purposes, the "uninterrupted" method allows greater integration of mind/body and movement. Constant flow is also essential to understanding the role of change in combat and in efficiently dealing with larger, heavier opponents.

The spirit ("shen") of t'ai chi form is drama of the most existential variety in that you "become" like the animals and birds whose movements you mimic in the various postures.

In the Chinese martial tradition, the eyes reflect the presence or lack of shen during t'ai chi practice. Westerners would be quick to admit that "the eyes are the windows of the soul." Martially, the eyes are trained through movement in the form and practice with a partner to act like laser sights. Your vision focuses narrowly only at the moment of attack so that you "lock on" to whatever part of the opponent you are attacking.

When linking t'ai chi and spirit, we are talking about an emotional intensity that is combined with a specific feel or energy. Such practice is choreography only in the sense that you are repeating a prearranged sequence of movements.

However, each time you perform the form (once you have mastered the technical details), you should feel as if it is the first time you've done it well. It's like making love—if you don't approach each session with the same partner with eagerness and total participation, you'll soon become bored and start looking for another partner or be content with occasionally going through the motions.

The modern masters of t'ai chi are unanimous on very few details of form practice. However, one they do agree on is the role of the eyes and spirit. Anyone who does form with the eyes half-closed or "dreamy" is *not* considered to be doing anything beyond going through the motions, even though those motions may be technically correct.

Even mediocre t'ai chi is worth doing, in some ways, but you have only to see a master performing beside the talented but uninvolved practitioner to see the difference in quality even though both may look superficially as if they're doing the same movements.

FITNESS BENEFITS

Regular performance of t'ai chi form in a moderate to deep

stance exercises the tissues connecting the muscles and skeletal structure. Such training gradually and moderately improves the sense of balance and increases flexibility while stimulating the flow of blood to the bones.

Increasing the supply of oxygen, minerals, and nutrients to the bone marrow helps that tissue in its production of the red and white corpuscles, which are essential factors in a healthy immune system.

In terms of heart/lung fitness, as defined by Western sports scientists, t'ai chi is a relatively mild form of exercise and has limitations in terms of developing those attributes most sought after by Western physical fitness advocates—muscular development and cardiovascular fitness.

The areas of the body that do tend to become strong are the upper legs, abdominal area, and torso. The rhythmic contractions of the abdominal area as you imagine breathing "into the belly" do strengthen and "elasticize" the muscle tone of the torso/abdominal area.

The eyes usually follow the movement of a hand or look ahead into the distance while doing form. As well as improving eye-hand coordination, this exercises those muscles which are responsible for adjusting focal length in the vision. Such exercise can actually improve eyesight for specific problems, especially in younger practitioners.

T'ai chi is perhaps of more use to the cardiovascular system than would be first apparent. Doing the form as if you were moving slowly through water provides an isotonic effect, which does stimulate muscle strength, especially in the legs and lower body.

The increased efficiency of the muscles of the lower body has a cardiovascular effect in that the valves and walls of the arteries and veins are assisted by the stronger muscles to circulate blood more efficiently to and from the heart. In addition, concepts of ch'i-flow aside, the deep breathing combined with the slow movement of form trains the body to use oxygen more efficiently.

However, it is misleading, as some instructors have claimed, to state that doing long form provides a low-impact aerobic workout. Competently doing slow form gives about the same cardiovascular workout as you would get from walking at a moderate pace for the same amount of time. Those forms done at a mixed or rapid pace can, of course, bring considerable benefit in terms of cardiovascular exercise.

Interestingly enough, in recent years, some scientific studies have indicated that long-term low- (walking) to moderate- (noncompetitive swimming/cycling) intensity workouts may actually be more beneficial in terms of decreasing the risk of premature death from stroke or heart disease than the high-intensity workouts (running or aerobics).

For example, a study published in 1990 by the *Journal of the American Medical Association* indicated that it is not necessary to reach for high levels of cardiovascular performance to benefit from such exercise.

It showed that the men who participated in the study over an eight-year period and maintained relatively low levels of cardiovascular fitness were less than half as likely to die as the sedentary participants of the study. The findings for women were similar. Researchers said that the findings were especially significant in that they linked the benefits of such exercise to a lower incidence of some types of cancer as well as heart disease.

The Taoists, in this way, may have been ahead of their time in prescribing their exercises as a way to healthy longevity while ridiculing those who advocated hard-style exertion that only benefited the muscles.

T'ai chi form practice can act as a means of biofeedback— without the need for expensive machinery to train yourself to recognize and release the symptoms of physical tension.

TRAINING "TRICKS" FOR FORM AND PRACTICE

The following training "tricks" can help create an awareness of the unique aspects of form practice. They can be used to help practitioners pay attention while training. Being "forced" to pay attention can create a physical/emotional climate conducive to an intuitive understanding.

Realigning the Body
It can be difficult to see ourselves as we really are. However, to

reform your posture through t'ai chi you must experience your posture as it is *now*. To get a feel for how you hold yourself, you need a full-length mirror and the assistance of a friend. Stand in front of the mirror and, without first having examined yourself, close your eyes. You should be wearing a bathing suit or skin-tight exercise gear so that you cannot hide behind baggy clothes.

With eyes still closed, assume the posture "central equilibrium" from the beginning of whatever style of t'ai chi you are learning. Do a few moments of standing meditation, then open your eyes and look at your reflection.

If you're like many people, you either have avoided looking in mirrors or have not really seen yourself as a totality. Look beyond the external cosmetic factors like the shape of the hips or the protruding belly, although these also should tell you something about yourself.

Is your head tilted back? Does your chin jut forward aggressively? Does your head lean to one side? Is one shoulder held slightly higher than the other? Do you lean back on the heels of the feet or tilt slightly forward on their balls? Is one hip held higher than the other? Do you throw more weight on one leg than on the other? Do your knees and feet splay in or out? How is your general alignment? Do you look tense or relaxed; poised or slumped?

As a future reference you could have a friend take your photo at the moment you open your eyes before you can become aware of and correct the gross errors that you see.

These photos should be from the front and in profile. Repeating the exercise and creating a photographic record at regular intervals (every six months) can give you a permanent record of your progress or lack thereof as your practice of form evolves.

You can repeat the process for any of the postures from form, although as static images they won't be an accurate reflection of how you are when moving from posture to posture. The use of a camcorder to film the same section of your form at six-month intervals will also give you a valuable reference of how your posture/skill-levels evolve over time. (Although I, for one, am just as happy not to have a film of myself performing the t'ai chi form that I taught myself from a Bruce Tegner book back in the early '70s!)

As a means of reintegrating posture, form should gently lead you first to become aware of your habitual posture and then slowly lead you into being more correct in terms of how you stand, sit, and exist. Is there really any benefit to your practice of t'ai chi if your posture is only relaxed and true to the classics when you are practicing form? Shouldn't the practice of form eventually lead to your posture being correct even when you aren't concentrating on it? This, of course, is usually a long-term process except for the very talented.

If you spent years (as I did) walking with your head tilted slightly to one side, one shoulder higher than the other and the weight of the body unevenly distributed onto the outside edges of the feet, you won't (and shouldn't) undo it overnight.

If you try to force the process of change, you may get seemingly quicker results but may also have months of pain as your body adjusts to being suddenly obliged to be the way it should have been.

Being Attentive

It can be difficult to experience "flow" as you do form. One way of learning to pay attention is to use audiotapes to accompany your form practice. You can either purchase a suitable tape (e.g., readings of the Taoist classics) or record your own preferences and then play them when doing form.

The sound level should be loud enough to hear clearly, but not blaring. However, doing form in a noisy environment is, in itself, an exercise in being attentive.

It's relatively easy to enter a meditative state of mind when practicing alone in a park or in a room by yourself, but more of a challenge when in the "real" world. If your t'ai chi only works under ideal conditions, can it have real value?

You should have a fundamental grasp of the mechanics of your form so that you don't have to constantly divide your attention between remembering where your hands and feet go and what you're listening to.

This process is not simply to create a pseudo-Oriental atmosphere for your practice or provide appropriate background noise. It is a means of focusing your attention on the theoretical/philosophical roots of the art as you do its physical expression, form.

Not surprisingly, it is difficult to blend listening attention with movement attention without detracting from either aspect. T'ai chi as a means of moving meditation should be an enhancement of your awareness of self and environment and not just some New Age trance state of blind introspection.

If you are using such tapes with friends or to teach, some consideration should be paid to the occasional student who feels that this kind of training aid—when it involves Taoist readings—may be a form of subliminal brainwashing. Not all students of t'ai chi want or are willing to accept the Taoist basis as being valid for them for either philosophical or religious reasons.

"Slowing" Down

With reference to the preceding section, musical backgrounds can be a means of experiencing how musical rhythms affect our personal rhythms. Many instructors are opposed to the use of music as a background to t'ai chi practice; a few feel that it can be very beneficial, notably the renowned T.T. Liang.

I like to play drum beats or intense folk music (Armenian, Greek, Irish) when sparring with weapons, as those rhythms really "get the juices flowing" in terms of realistic applications. Slow, gentle rhythms help to slow your pace of performing form. New Age, some Oriental (e.g., Japanese flute) and nature/environmental sound recordings are effective. Avoid rock music!

If you have difficulty slowing down your form to the time required by your style and the length of form being done, use a timer. I recommend the electronic version, as they are generally more accurate and beep loudly so you don't miss the signal.

To begin, do the form and check the elapsed time when you are done. Don't get too depressed if you did long form in twelve minutes! The next time you practice set the timer to ring at the thirteen-minute mark. If you finish before the alarm goes, try again on subsequent days. At some point you will "beat the clock." Then increase the time to fourteen minutes and go for that.

In this way you can gradually build to doing the form slowly enough to always end at approximately the time the alarm sounds. Once you can do that with consistency, you won't need the timer.

Conclusion

Long-term study is necessary to see any lasting physical, emotional, spiritual, or martial benefits in terms of form training. It is essential to practice every day, and preferably a long rather than a short or simplified form.

Sadly, as t'ai chi becomes more and more popular, it is becoming harder and harder to find instruction in long form. Most beginners, North American and Chinese alike, have neither the interest, time, nor patience to attempt such study.

Some styles and instructors advocate doing a mirror-image of the form to develop all postures equally on both sides of the body. My personal feeling is in accord with that of Ch'eng Man-ching, who felt that since people were, by nature, either right- or left-handed, it would imbalance them to put too much effort into learning form equally well on both sides.

After doing form you should feel both tired *and* energized. If you feel only one way, then either your practice or instruction is flawed. It is also important to remember that doing the form competently can, by itself, take months or years to achieve.

The time spent as a beginner is, in a sense, neither energetic nor therapeutic, although it provides the foundation for such practice. Even when beyond the beginner stage, if you do form listlessly, mechanically, or unimaginatively, you will end up with minimal benefits.

Too little is just as bad as too much effort. The Taoistic basis of t'ai chi emphasizes *moderation,* and the desired result is to create and maintain health into old age as well as provide the basis for self-defense skills that don't depend on the factors linked to strength and youth.

It can be difficult to develop a true appreciation of the value of form practice. For example, for many years I devoted much less effort to it than to the interactive and martial aspects of t'ai chi. It's only been in the last few years that I've grown to really appreciate why form practice is an *essential* half of the art, no matter what your level of expertise.

That said, it is also true that, having absorbed the principles of t'ai chi, you eventually no longer need to practice form as much as you did when you were at a beginner or intermediate level. However, deciding when you have reached this point is very subjective and is best left up to your instructor(s).

It's easy to fool yourself as to your level of expertise when practicing on your own—no matter how many years you have been training. Paradoxically, it is equally true that the solo practice, by itself, will not automatically bring martial skill. Never let anyone convince you that it is possible to develop self-defense skills by simply doing form—even ten years of superb form practice can't bring such skills unless you have trained with others as well.

Ch'i (also chi or qi in English) is that mysterious force, or intrinsic energy, that defines existence. While the theory of ch'i and its cultivation are well-established in China, the Western understanding of intrinsic energy is still in its infancy.

On a pragmatic level, such energy is only immediately understood when absent—those of you who have seen a human or animal cadaver have probably not confused death with sleep. Without ch'i, bodies, no matter how fresh, are reduced to mere husks.

When talking of this vital force one generally thinks of living things, but according to traditional Taoist thought (and modern physics), all aspects of existence—even the non-living—are composed of various manifestations of this energy. For example, the earth is said to have ch'i which circulates along specific pathways called "dragon veins." The quality of such energy, depending on the location, can either be harmful or beneficial to living things.

Even Westerners talk about a geographical loca-

CHAPTER 5

CH'I FOR HEALING AND COMBAT

tion giving a good or bad feeling. Whether or not this is caused by the presence (or absence) of ch'i or some form of emotional prejudice (e.g., a room is painted a color you hate) is immaterial to choosing wisely. Some locations, perhaps as a result of where they are situated or of having accumulated energy from those using them, feel right for training; others don't.

Traditionally, parks, wooded areas, and mountains were said to be the best sources of environmental ch'i; early morning and late evening the best times to train. Some t'ai chi classes feel better than others, and it may well be, in part, the times at which the classes are held that helps or hinders the learning process.

Even Western scientists are devoting more research to human biological cycles to discover why we are, for example, more creative at certain times of the day, month, or season.

While it is relatively easy to intellectualize the subject, it is not so easy to define it on a personal level. My own feeling is that an intrinsic energy—let's call it ch'i—exists and, given competent effort and instruction, can be cultivated for both health and martial purposes.

The beneficial therapeutic use of acupuncture (insertion of metal needles at various points on the skin, with or without the accompanying use of mild electrical charges) demonstrates that something is going on that cannot totally be explained from a pragmatic viewpoint. Acupuncture has been used successfully on domestic animals, and a horse cannot be sedated or freed from pain because it has faith in the procedure.

However, becoming attuned to ch'i is not a question of trying to master or control it, although you frequently come across such approaches. Trying to control ch'i is like damming a turbulent river: the effort may seem successful at first, but it may also cause harmful and unexpected drainage or flooding problems.

This need for control, for personal "power," is partly the result of human nature and partly due to our having become disconnected from our role in nature. It's only in the last few years that man has begun, through the efforts of environmentalists, to realize that we are not separate from or in command of nature. Everything we do as individuals and as a species has an effect on nature and, in turn, on our existence. (Unfortunately, the environmental movement is largely motivated by fear and self-preservation—not that those aren't valid factors—as opposed to a psychological/spiritual feeling of connection with nature, with ch'i. It should not be a source of consolation that the Chinese and Japanese, despite their Taoist and Shinto heritages, have been just as wanton in terms of polluting their respective ecosystems.)

You are already full of ch'i in that existence is defined and permeated by it. On an individual level, learning to work with the ch'i is very much a process of *becoming aware* of how its manifestations affect you to balance its internal flow, if such balancing is needed.

Recent efforts to study ch'i on the Chinese mainland and in North America are helping to make traditional explanations more meaningful to Westerners. For example, Dr. Yang Jwing-Ming, a t'ai chi instructor in Boston, has done much research on the subject and, as a result, feels that ch'i is a biomechanical electrical force that can be cultivated through many of the traditional exercises.

Such exercises have survived in the Taoist writings or been handed down by word of mouth over the generations. Dr. Yang's views on ch'i and interpretations of the traditional training methods are a remarkable attempt to explain ch'i in scientific terms.

While the Chinese government has also expended a great deal of effort and money on ch'i research, its results have been, in some ways, "overenthusiastic" from a pragmatic point of view. In addition, their conclusions have not always been replicated under more rigorous experimental conditions in North America.

In contrast to such approaches, many t'ai chi teachers insist on the importance of unquestioningly accepting the traditional theories behind ch'i and its cultivation. And many Westerners are sadly eager to accept ch'i as a magical cure-all for their physical and emotional ills because they have lost faith in Western science.

However, defining ch'i empirically is of less value, in pragmatic terms, than knowing if cultivating it through t'ai chi or related exercises will improve your health and martial skills. To use a modern example, scientists are still not quite sure why Acetylsalicylic Acid (ASA) has such a wide range of medical applications, but it does.

Of course, one can have too much blind faith, and ASA, like other drugs, can have negative effects on the health of some people (as can the study of ch'i). However, it is only necessary to know *whether* it works for the average individual when properly "taken" under normal conditions, not *why* in exhaustive detail!

You must also remember that taking a pill which you think is Acetylsalicylic Acid will often alleviate your pain even when the tablet is really only sugar. The placebo affect is well-documented in Western medicine and is an important factor in any healing process.

Whether or not ch'i and its cultivation are largely forms of self-hypnosis or are objectively real as the traditionalists would have us believe is, in large measure, immaterial to whether or not it can be beneficial.

As in all aspects of training you have to have faith, and it may well be that faith, by itself, is ch'i.

There are symptoms of being attuned to ch'i flow: feelings of warmth, tingling of the skin, and other sensory phenomena. However, such manifestations should not be confused with having "mastered" ch'i. If, as a beginner, you have been told by an authority exactly what you will experience, it would be very surprising if you did *not* experience such phenomena.

It is better to approach such work with little coaching on details of what you will experience. Then if you get such symptoms, you will know that they come because of the training, not because of some form of autosuggestion. In many ways, the physical symptoms are simply signs that you are becoming aware of things you should never have lost touch with in the first place.

Many of the the best instructors are fervent believers in ch'i and its cultivation; however, others, equally respected and skilled, believe that it has little relevance to modern students. At some point, it is essential for the serious t'ai chi practitioner to develop, at the least, an intellectual understanding of ch'i as well as a feeling of how he or she wishes to incorporate (or ignore) it in training.

CH'I-KUNG

The following discussion is a *simplified introduction* to the basic concepts of ch'i and its cultivation. Like any other body of knowledge, there are many interpretations of specific details, depending on the source consulted.

In traditional terms, we are born with prenatal ch'i, whose quality was determined by genetic factors. As we grow, we slowly use it up (much as the embryo in an egg uses the protein-rich fluid that surrounds it in the shell to mature), partially replacing it with postnatal ch'i.

The latter is also called "acquired" ch'i and is made up of air, water, food, and environmental ch'i. All these can be transmuted by the use of physical and mental effort to higher forms of energy. These higher forms are a "distillation" of the baser forms of energy and are sought for health, martial, and spiritual reasons.

Ch'i is stored largely in the kidneys and the lower, physical tan tien, the Ch'i Hai (or "Sea of Ch'i"), located slightly below and behind the navel. As a large ch'i "reservoir" is considered to have spiritual implications, many of the Taoist religious figures are depicted as being pear-shaped and laughing with inner joy. (By contrast, joy is a rather rare concept in Christian and Buddhist traditions. The religious figures of the former, in particular, are usually depicted as being lean, if not actually gaunt. Fortunately, there are exceptions—one has only to think of the round benevolence of Saint Nicholas to realize that such notions are not totally alien to the West.)

Ch'i courses through channels, the meridian network, in the body as well as smaller conduits ("lou") that nourish the tissues and bone marrow with ch'i and are connected to the outside world by means of specific points near the skin surface.

The meridians connect five pairs of organs. Each pair is a yin and yang dichotomy, and each pair is also affected by interaction of the five elements (fire, earth, metal, water, wood) and eight "vessels," of which four are very important: the Triple-Heater, Heart-Constrictor, Governing, and Conception vessels.

As examples of the interaction of the organs, meridians, and vessels, the Triple-Heater is said to control respiration, internal temperature, and the urinary/genital tract, the Heart-Constrictor controls the energy of the circulatory system and the kidneys and is related to sexual energy.

In some ways, the two most important vessels are the Governing (Du Mei) and the Conception (Ren Mei), which are said (when the tongue is held up against the roof of the mouth) to trace a spiritually energizing, closed circuit around the front and back of the torso and head—the Grand Circulation. This connects the Hui Yin point on the perineum at the base of the torso to the Bai Hui point on the crown of the head.

One of the objectives of cultivating the ch'i is to make it follow the dictates of the mind ("I") through sinking the breath to the lower tan tien where it mixes with the sexual secretions and is transformed into internal force (ch'ing, also spelled "jing" or "ching").

There are, again, different varieties and qualities of ch'ing, and these can be circulated for a variety of purposes, at will, to any point of the body or, at high levels of skill, outside it. With great effort, ch'i and ch'ing can, it is said, be further refined through certain meditative practices and physical exercises to eventually create an internal "elixir" of refined energy that (depending on which Taoist sects you believe) brings either a spiritual or physical immortality or both.

A blockage or lessening of the flow of ch'i and ch'ing (due, among other factors, to stress, physical tension, poor diet, environmental factors, and shallow breathing) can cause sickness, both mental and physical. One of the first principles of an internal martial art, or ch'i-kung, is to relieve and balance the internal flow of energy.

You can, for discussion purposes, think of yourself as a rechargeable ch'i "battery." If you are overused and not plugged into a source of energy, you'll *quickly* lose your charge. However, if you aren't used, you'll *slowly* lose the ability to take and hold a charge. On the other hand, if you become obsessed with yourself and with practices like ch'i-kung, you can also overcharge and burn yourself out! Philosophical Taoism advocates moderation and balance. If one is already ill, especially if fever is present, it is best to avoid exertion and practice only the mild forms such as standing or sitting meditation. While there are very effective forms of therapeutic ch'i-kung for certain conditions, these must be prescribed and *supervised* by an expert. There is great wisdom in the old adage, "He who doctors himself has a fool for a physician."

Active and Passive Ch'i-Kung

The soft styles of ch'i-kung (those emphasizing health) fall into two major categories: active and passive.

Active is characterized by an emphasis on abdominal breathing in conjunction with bodily movements and mental effort designed to direct the ch'i to circulate throughout the body. T'ai chi ch'uan is thus an active form of ch'i-kung.

Passive ch'i-kung makes use of breathing, mental effort, and static postures in either a reclining, sitting, kneeling, or standing position. Sitting meditation is thus a passive form of ch'i-kung.

In both active and passive forms, the breathing process is very important. Learning to breathe deeply promotes spiritual calmness ("inner quiet") as well as physical relaxation. In the *Tao Te Ching*, Lao Tzu asks that you "regulate the breath, becoming soft and pliant like an infant."

The physical aspects of active ch'i-kung relax and improve the physical condition of the torso and the internal organs through gentle stretching and the practitioner becoming aware, on an ongoing basis, of his internal condition.

Most of those interested in fitness or the martial arts are overly concerned with stretching and relaxing the limbs but neglect to train the internal organs to relax and move as part of a holistic process—balancing the flow of energy in the body/mind; relaxing the connective tissue throughout the body, not just in the limbs; and unifying the three spiritual centers (those that correspond to the abdomen, heart, and mind).

Many t'ai chi instructors believe that properly executed *long* form balances and improves ch'i flow and that paying too much attention to ch'i development is as counterproductive as ignoring it completely.

Regulating this energy for martial and self-healing purposes is also accomplished through standing meditation ("chan-kung"), in which t'ai chi or other postures are held for variable amounts of time.

Some of the t'ai chi postures (e.g., Golden Cock) will be more challenging physically than others (e.g., central equilibrium), and you should increase the amount of time spent holding the more difficult postures *gradually*.

It is physically impossible to hold all but the easiest postures for any length of time if you allow yourself to be tense and fail to empty the mind of random or obsessive thoughts, and unless you pay attention to the breathing process. If you persevere, your mind and body will eventually be forced to learn how to let go of unnecessary muscle tension in order to relieve the discomfort.

Ch'i-kung has become very popular in recent years, and many instructors are insisting that t'ai chi form practice must be supplemented by one or more methods of ch'i-kung training. A significant number feel that t'ai chi is *not* a form of ch'i-kung (if you define it strictly as a means of improving health), as it is too martial. For them, the practice of other exercises is necessary to gain the maximum health benefits.

It is up to you to decide for yourself in terms of your own needs whether or not you should supplement your t'ai chi practice with other forms of ch'i-kung. However, I firmly believe that you should avoid imagining the circulation of the breath and/or ch'i along the various meridians or internal paths during such exercise unless a qualified instructor has helped you to determine that you need and will benefit from such intensive practice and shown you how to go about it safely.

In some ways the most important factor in coming to such a decision is whether or not ongoing, competent instruction is readily available. *Reading a few books, watching a video, or attending a workshop will not necessarily give you the tools to practice safely on your own!*

For example, as ch'i-kung makes great use of breath control, such practices may raise the possibility of adversely affecting the chemical balance in the brain, as can be done through intentional or accidental hyperventilation or breath-holding.

Altering the brain's chemical state can kill cells, dangerously affect blood pressure levels, and cause emotional stress and hallucinations. Similarly, you must be very careful never to force the breathing in a misguided effort to actually breathe "through the abdomen." Swallowing air into the digestive system will only give you gas, at best.

Inhaled air cannot be carried to the abdomen except as oxygen which has been integrated into the bloodstream by the action of the lungs.

The lungs themselves are very elastic, but they can be overworked. Any sudden pain in the chest region or feeling of constriction can be the symptom of nervous tension or straining of the organs, muscles, or connective tissues of the torso.

There were Taoist sects who believed that physical immortality could be achieved if the practitioner learned to forego the necessity for breathing. To do this, they practiced holding the breath for progressively longer periods of time. Of course, at a certain point in such training, the chemical levels in the brain become so affected that hallucinations and unconsciousness can develop. For those fanatics who believed that the resultant hallucinations were manifestations of creating a "spiritual double of themselves" and of "flying on the dragon's wings," the eventual result was brain damage as they overcame the protective mechanism of losing consciousness, which automatically allows the body to resume respiration when deprived of oxygen.

Some such extreme ch'i-kung practices have survived (even if their originators have not) and should be avoided. Too many fanatics hide such failures behind the rationalization that if tragedy occurs, the cause is not the practice but "lack of faith" on the part of the beginner.

Consider the parable, variations of which appear in many spiritual teaching traditions, of the man who was anxious to reduce the cost of maintaining his donkey. Each day he would diminish the amount of feed given the poor beast—which he continued to work as before. Inevitably, it wasted away and died. Distraught, the owner complained to his neighbors that the stupid animal had died just at the point where he had almost trained it to go completely without food.

The classics say, "put stress on the spirit, not the ch'i. Too much preoccupation on ch'i results in stagnation." Symptoms of improper or dangerous ch'i-kung practice include: unusual feelings of cold, sudden pain or numbness, frightening visual and/or auditory hallucinations, involuntary body movement that does not subside immediately when you cease practicing, convulsions or tremors, sudden or unusual hair loss, headache, and nausea/vomiting.

Sexual Ch'i-Kung

Before beginning a discussion of a controversial subject, it is important to remember that the Chinese have never had a cultural obsession with minimizing or rejecting the sensual world as has often been the case in both Christian and Buddhist societies.

For certain Taoists, a variety of sexual practices were and still are used as a form of ch'i-kung for health, spiritual, and martial (and marital) purposes. The sexual fluids of the male and female practitioners are considered essential to the transmutation of ch'i and ch'ing to more subtle, refined energies.

Of particular concern for male practitioners is the retention of semen except for purposes of procreation, especially in older men. The loss of semen is considered a literal loss of vital energy—a loss which becomes more and more threatening to the life span if done to excess in later years.

Conversely, sexual activities leading to orgasm without male ejaculation while encouraging female orgasm were sought as a means of increasing the quality and quantity of ch'i in both partners. Certain Taoist sects have also used forms of self-massage, which could also be called masturbation, as a means of meditation/energy cultivation.

In some Taoist sects, women have used certain exercises, meditative practices, and dietary restrictions to cause a cessation of menstruation. Such loss of body fluids was, like male ejaculation, considered to be a loss of vital energy. Stopping the natural cycle in young women occurs naturally in times of caloric deprivation or as a result of overtraining physically, as with female athletes. The hormonal balance necessary for a normal menstrual cycle is partially dependent on the amount of body fat present and the dietary intake. Such a cessation should not automatically be interpreted as a sign of greater spiritual development!

In terms of the connection between ch'i and the internal martial arts (including t'ai chi ch'uan), the dividing line between sexual and aggressive energies is tenuous, and not just for the Chinese. In ancient times, the Roman gladiator combats were popular with prostitutes, who converged on the arenas after the games because they knew that business would be particularly brisk with those who had just been watching the bloodletting. And, they reasoned, the turnover of clients would be faster than normal because of increased levels of arousal. In more modern times, Western boxers and athletes were, until comparatively recently, advised by their coaches and colleagues to refrain from intercourse before a competition or fight, as the sexual activity and loss of sperm were believed to affect the energy levels adversely.

You can easily carry the analogy between human behavior and that of the animal world too far; however, it is tempting to see a correlation between the combat among male animals over a female in season to decide who will copulate with her and the arousal many men (and women) feel during and after having watched or participated in contact sports or violence.

While there is a great deal of truth in the feminist theories about the relationship between sexual violence and the male need to dominate and subjugate women, rape is such a prevalent accompaniment to warfare partly because men seem biologically predisposed to find violence arousing.

There is no doubt that some aspects of the internal arts are sexually stimulating, especially when done with a partner. Whether or not this was noticed long ago and rationalized through being fitted into the Taoist framework is impossible to determine and largely immaterial to the fact that sex, ch'i-kung, and the internal martial arts are bed partners. It may also be that, as one famous t'ai chi instructor said, "People like to have sex, and this is as good an excuse as any!"

Sexual ch'i-kung can be a potent form of energy cultivation; however, it is particularly liable to abuse by both teacher and student. It can be both an energizing and relaxing experience or an unsatisfying expression of neurotic needs. Both parties must willingly and honestly enter into such a relationship and be aware that emotional considerations can easily intrude and debase the practices or ruin the teacher-student relationship.

Let me be blunt—I have both known and heard of teachers who used such training, without believing in it as a form of ch'i-kung, as a way of ensuring a plentiful variety of sexual partners. It bears repeating that each participant must be very sure of his or her own motives and those of a partner before entering into an experience which can have severe side effects (sexually transmitted disease, pregnancy, emotional upset, and broken relationships).

Experienced and legitimate instructors in such practices are few and far between, even in the Orient. If you want to explore this form of ch'i-kung, you may have to resort to the books and videos available on the subject: James McNeil and Mantak Chia, among others, are respected authorities on the subject.

Certain practices advocated by New Age as well as traditional Taoists are more suited to the sadomasochistic than the average student. No matter whom you learn from, use common sense when being advised to indulge in practices that may cause biological damage or infection (e.g., hanging progressively heavier weights from the male genitals or inserting herbal formulae and various devices into the female genitalia).

MARTIAL USES OF CH'I

The use of ch'i for martial purposes falls into two categories: defensive and offensive.

The defensive side of it lies in those training methods which develop localized concentrations of energy—iron-shirt techniques—designed to strengthen the torso and limbs to render them relatively immune to attack.

Such concepts are not unique to the internal systems and have been used by Indian Yogis to lie on beds of nails, Polynesian priests to walk on beds of live coals, and hard-style boxers to have blocks of concrete resting on their abdomens shattered with sledge hammers. In a sense, such stunts are just tricks performed by skilled and experienced showmen; however, they are also legitimate examples of ch'i use—especially if you define ch'i as mind power.

Iron-shirt training is a very valuable tool for the martial artist, as he or she no longer needs to be overly concerned about being struck anywhere except the genitals or head. However, in modern times it has less value than it did in "the good old days." Remember that the cream of Chinese fighters were shot down during the Boxer Rebellion in China, despite their training.

The offensive use of ch'i training is called Tsien Hueh ("Vital

Spotting") or Dim-Mak ("Death-Hand") and involves interfering with the energy flow of an opponent. Such striking, twisting, squeezing, or a combination of those techniques can have an adverse affect on certain targets in the human body that would seem out of proportion to the effort made and the target.

Depending on the style being studied, there are said to be some 108 points along the meridians at which it is possible for a practitioner to interfere with the flow of ch'i through physical force and, at high levels of accomplishment, by transmitting his or her own ch'i into the victim, causing ill health, paralysis (temporary or otherwise), or even death. It is also important to remember that the meridians connect parts of the body that are not obvious on the surface. Thus the ch'i flowing through a series of points on the foot and leg may affect the heart or spleen when attacked precisely so as to adversely affect the flow of energy to and from a particular organ.

Depending on which sources you believe, the nervous and circulatory systems and the ch'i system are either one and the same or related but not completely synonymous. In any case, some examples of attacking the points more clearly affect nerve impulses and/or the blood circulatory system, while others are less clearly definable as to how they work so well from a physical perspective.

An example of the latter is the apparent "push" that ends the Grasp Bird's Tail posture. This was originally a double strike to certain meridian points near the shoulders. When the force applied is a spiraling/concussive energy rather than a blunt impact, the result can be equally out of proportion to the amount of force used and the apparent target.

By contrast, striking the solar plexus, from which nerves radiate to all parts of the torso, in the region of the sternum can have a martial effect out of proportion to the apparent force of the impact, as it can temporarily or permanently interrupt the rhythm of the heart. However, the results are hardly mysterious from a medical point of view. Police and correctional officers in some jurisdictions have, in the past, been criticized for using a pumping palm strike to the sternum to literally stop the heart of troublesome prisoners or suspects. Such attacks can leave little or no bruising. In most victims, the heart will subsequently start up again, either on its own or through CPR; however, for a minority with diagnosed or undiagnosed heart problems, it won't! You can't tell from looking at someone whether or not he or she falls into the "safe" category in terms of such strikes.

By contrast, the use of Dim-Mak is clouded by myth and built around elaborate theories of when and how to strike certain points to achieve the most lethal results, which may be immediate or in a few days or weeks. Such tactics are best suited to assassins and criminals, as there are few advantages, in terms of self-defense, to having your attacker drop dead three days after he's taken a poke at you! The only conclusive evidence of its existence is the fact that people have been injured or killed by contact that seemed casual and ineffective to those observing.

It would seen reasonable, with hindsight, to attribute some of these incidents to the attacker having knowingly or unknowingly caused internal injuries to an opponent. For example, a relatively light blow to the colon or bladder can rupture those organs, releasing irritants and toxins into the abdominal area. The victim may feel little or no initial pain, but hours or days later will die from peritoneal infection. However, in other cases, whether or not the victims were harmed because they *believed* in the existence of Dim-Mak and willed themselves to suffer is another question—one not easily answered.

In any case, even if you are able to find an instructor who can or claims to be able to teach such skills, you should question his and your motives for learning tactics that only have one use—grievously harming others. On a moral level, it is one thing to defend yourself with appropriate force and quite another to cause severe injury or death hours or days after the incident takes place.

Even though I have a professional curiosity about this aspect of ch'i manipulation, I am also glad that I know relatively little about it. Such skills development may have had moral relevance when created, but it has little place in modern life.

Instructors like Erle Montaigue teach certain aspects of this "evil knowledge" to the martial arts public only to help dispel some of the myths about it and demonstrate how important it is *not* to practice such tactics in a haphazard manner.

One can learn all the skills necessary for ethical self-defense without specializing in such skills. The use of ch'i in the internal arts should restore and promote good health, not destroy it.

In the last few years, there has been a healthy trend in both North America and China in terms of a return to the practice of the interactive side of t'ai chi: rooting/uprooting, push-hands (tui-shou), and four-corners (da-lu). This has been partly due to the interest in t'ai chi as a sport.

Competition demands that a participant train intensively to develop the self-assurance to demonstrate his or her skills in public. This, without a doubt, has value, and the growing enthusiasm for such events has helped to spread and popularize the art. However, the desirability of making t'ai chi a sport remains controversial. It is equally true that training to compete can dilute the health-building and martial aspects of the art in favor of performance skills—those which please judges and allow safe competition.

Whatever your feelings about t'ai chi as a sport, the traditional interactive exercises and a variety of related sensitivity-training methods are essential for the practitioner who wishes to

CHAPTER 6

MARTIAL FUNDAMENTALS

refine his or her understanding of the benefits and applications of solo form practice.

Such training teaches the proper interaction of the "thirteen postures" as expressed through individual applications as well as in tui-shou and da-lu. Their internalization remains the cornerstone of the interactive side of t'ai chi, although it is possible to place too much value on them, as is done in some schools.

Even if you have no interest in learning t'ai chi as a martial art or system of self-defense, it is still preferable to try such training methods for a period of time. Even a relatively short taste of the interactive side of the art will better help you appreciate what processes occur within you when doing the solo form.

THE THIRTEEN POSTURES

The traditional thirteen postures consist of the "eight actions" (ward-off, roll-back, press, push, pull-down, split, elbow stroke, and shoulder stroke) performed within the "five directions" (look to the left, look to the right, advance, retreat, and central equilibrium).

The importance of the thirteen postures lies in the relationship between the actions and directions. To clarify, it is not whether you do a technically competent posture that matters as much as how well you internalize its action/reaction and how smoothly and spontaneously you can respond to a training partner's size, intent, and action.

If an instructor claims to be teaching the interactive and/or self-defense side of the art and the thirteen postures are not a prominent part of the curriculum, you're not learning t'ai chi. It may be valid as a martial exercise, but it isn't the real thing.

The Eight Actions
These movements are effective both as training tools and as combative tactics—if applied correctly and with spirit.

◆ *Ward-off (peng)* can be used defensively as an acceptance of an opponent's incoming force and a "bouncing" return of it. While it is usually expressed through a forearm (as if the practitioner were holding an invisible shield in front of the body), it can also be applied with any part of the body at high levels of skill. Offensively, it can be used to strike vulnerable areas while simultaneously invading the opponent's space.

◆ *Roll-back (lu)* is accomplished by sticking to an incoming force and deflecting it to one side and behind you by turning the waist/torso and shifting the weight. While deflecting, you can also use roll-back to dislocate the elbow or shoulder or to throw your partner off balance by using the arm to which you've "stuck" as a lever/fulcrum.

◆ *Press (chi)* can be used to move someone who is strongly rooted, provide a double-impact strike (one palm collapsing into the other as if you were flattening a ball of energy held between the hands), or to squeeze an upward or downward "scissoring" of energy into the heart region.

◆ *Push (an)* is a double-handed push using either the front or back leg (depending on which authority you follow) as a power base. It is also a spiral, pulsating strike into certain acupuncture points on the shoulders. If the shoulders seem like a stupid target, you've never had the "thrill" of being pushed by someone who knows how and where to apply energy. In addition, a palm strike/push can be a very effective means of stopping a punch if your timing is correct. You target the shoulder connected to the incoming fist. This application works best against someone whose reach is less than or roughly equal to your own.

◆ *Pull-down (tsai)* is a whiplash energy directed sharply downward to affect the joints of the limb being pulled and the spine, especially the neck. It is most clearly seen in Needle at the Sea Bottom, a technique in which you whiplash the neck and dislocate the wrist/elbow while simultaneously effecting a release of a grip on your wrist. The follow-through action also positions you to strike into the crotch (the Sea Bottom, as in the Ch'i Hai or Sea of Ch'i).

◆ *Split (lieh)* is the most obvious manifestation of the tendency for forces in t'ai chi to be applied simultaneously in at least two different directions at once. Hands Strum the Lute demonstrates this action as a spraining/breaking action against the elbow joint. Slanting Flying posture demonstrates its use as a means of striking under the armpit while simultaneously throwing your opponent across the knee of your lead leg.

◆ *Elbow stroke (chou)* can be used defensively to save the elbow by supporting it with the free hand when pressure is applied against the joint. Offensively, it is a "folding" tactic if your hand is parried or blocked from the outside. It is a useful close-in tactic and is particularly effective against specific acupuncture points on the sides of the knees in countering leg attacks and against the upper arms in taking the fight out of an opponent's hand techniques.

◆ *Shoulder stroke (kao)* is an extremely potent weapon against someone who pulls you toward him instead of deflecting your forward movement. It is another aspect of folding in that you can shoulder if your elbow stroke is parried to one side. It is particularly effective against the heart region or if you can simultaneously stretch and lock an arm while shouldering it or the attached shoulder joint.

Both elbow and shoulder strokes are best accomplished when your opponent initiates the momentum for them. For example, you are less likely to connect with a shoulder stroke if you try to step or lunge forward. Being pulled and accepting that invitation with your body are the best ways to do these two actions—especially if you are much smaller than your opponent.

◆ *Palm slap* is a neutralization/strike hidden within each of the previous actions. A proper slap must come from the waist and be done when your palm has "stuck" to the target. It is much less effective when motivated by the shoulder as opposed to the waist. A proper slap to the face is very hard on the neck vertebrae of the person struck and should be used with discretion, especially when training.

The Five Directions

◆ *Look to the left.* In t'ai chi classics, it is an axiom that *initially* you go in the opposite direction of where you want to end up. So if my partner attacks from the right or the front, I can move to the left to begin my neutralization or redirection of the oncoming force so that I can return it in the form of one of the eight actions.

◆ *Look to the right.* Similarly, if the attack comes from the front or the left, you should first neutralize to the right before returning the attacking energy in the form of one of the eight actions. As in look to the left, the actual physical movement need not be with footwork. It may be very small—a slight turning of the waist seemingly in the opposite direction to which you need to respond—but it must be present.

◆ *Advance.* In general, your intention should always be to move forward when your partner retreats so that you are emotionally/spiritually penetrating not only his defense but the physical space he is occupying. (A minority of instructors argue that the classics have been mistranslated and that you must move forward immediately against any forward attack and not follow if the other person retreats. Such strategy works well if you are well-trained in it and not much lighter in weight than your partner or opponent.)

◆ *Retreat.* Paradoxically, when seeming to move back while under pressure, you must continue to "feel" as if you are advancing. Retreats quickly become routs if the person withdrawing panics or lets himself be overwhelmed by a larger, more aggressive partner.

◆ *Central equilibrium.* This is the most important direction even though it is as much a spiritual feeling as it is a physical direction. To have central equilibrium is to be filled with "inner quiet" when in movement and with the potential for supple and dynamic action when at rest. The form itself is a metaphor for this concept. You begin with the stillness of central equilibrium, flow from one posture to another, and return to it. In metaphysical terms, it is as if you never began, as if you never stopped.

Many martial artists talk of creating this centering and understanding of internal energy, but few actually do. When someone who can do it begins a t'ai chi form, the quality of that form is revealed immediately. I used to think it was arrogant of some of the experts I have met to stop watching someone demonstrate his form after the first few movements. But with experience you realize that a person's internal skill is either there in the *first* move of his form or not at all. (Nevertheless, common courtesy demands that one at least pretend to pay attention to a "lifeless" performance—not ignore it or read a book!)

Rooting, Uprooting, and Pushing

True rooting implies an ongoing physical/psychological sinking to lower the center of gravity and get a better feel for your own balance as you move or remain in place. Proper uprooting implies that your rooting is superior to your opponent's.

When "push comes to shove," as the saying goes, you are better off with competency at rooting than uprooting, as the former gives you balance and stability without sacrificing speed of reaction time and the ability to change. Conversely, uprooting is useful in the sense of keeping your opponent off-balance but less useful if it is viewed chiefly as being part of a good push. However, it does teach you to discharge energy safely without losing your balance.

The worldwide trend in the last few years of having competition in push-hands has increased the risk of students placing too much emphasis on rooting, sticking, and pushing so that they become ends in themselves as opposed to simply exercises that teach important skills *when studied in the proper context.*

Even the variable tempo and unpredictable exchanges of free-style push-hands fall short of the realism of self-defense training. Erle Montaigue and a few other instructors have braved considerable criticism by questioning the fanatical emphasis many instructors place on fixed-step pushing/uprooting skills.

There is a Sufi fable concerning the boatman who was rowing a philosopher across a wide lake. The philosopher asked the boatman if he knew anything about the wonders of abstract thought. The latter admitted that he did not.

"Ah then," sniffed the philosopher contemptuously, "you have wasted half of your life."

A little while later a freak wave swamped their small craft, which began to sink immediately. The boatman asked his passenger if the latter knew how to swim. "I never bothered to learn!" was the fearful reply.

"Ah then," called the boatman over his shoulder as he dived smoothly into the water, "you have wasted the rest of your life!"

An effective push is only "half a life" in that you are usually reacting to being held in some way, and such tactics are not likely to be encountered in competition (because they are usually banned) or on the street (because they only work if the attacker is much bigger than the victim and/or highly skilled at grappling). That's why releasing and folding techniques are so essential to the repertoire of a t'ai chi player. If you allow a hand or arm to be held (and I'm not necessarily talking about joint-locking of any kind), you limit your ability to use the waist or move your feet.

Acceptance, "going with the flow," is as integral to the t'ai chi experience as it was to the Taoists of legend and history. It is essential to an understanding of noninterference (wu-wei). Accepting the reality of incoming force is essential if you are to redirect it (as opposed to confronting it).

With time, the practice of t'ai chi with a variety of partners of different sizes and experience levels can help you learn to let go of the emotional need to control what will happen to you. The impossibility of controlling life is clearly demonstrated when one tries to plan ahead of receiving the actual push.

If you resist in life, you succeed only in creating tension, which, by itself, tends to further tension and results in ill health. On the other hand, not resisting in the sense of going limp means that you are simply being swept away by the tide of events instead of using the flow of energy to your own ends. Either extreme is equally bad.

Aside from the spiritual/emotional benefits, "standing meditation" (picking a posture from form and holding it for a *minimum* of five minutes) is one way of developing a root, developing the feeling of ch'i flow, and learning how to relax physically.

Even five minutes can seem like an agonizing eternity unless you use *just* the right amount of muscle to hold your arms and legs where they should be. With time, such practice will make you feel "heavy" and stable.

In terms of uprooting and sensitivity development, you can also do t'ai chi ball exercises with a partner as a variation of empty-hands uprooting. Use a hollow plastic ball with a diameter of about a foot. The ball should be firm but springy to the touch.

Both partners hold the ball between them with both hands (the stance doesn't matter). You each try to get possession of the sphere and make the other let go of it while losing his balance and/or moving his feet. You can move only if pulled and can also use the ball (but not the hands) to push your partner.

Such an exercise is a lot of fun and surprisingly tricky to do, even if you resort to forcing—which is easy. Being stiff and aggressive during such exercises is as counterproductive as being overly limp and passive.

It bears repeating that you must not confuse understanding such methods with developing self-defense skills. Push-hands are basic aspects of a process of growth which has at least three plateaus: learning the mechanics of movement, understanding how they relate to the principles, and, finally, applying those principles on a spontaneous basis.

If you can't push properly, you won't be able to use t'ai chi principles, although you may still be able to stick, deflect, and return incoming energy. Conversely, having an awesome push does not necessarily mean that you will be able to defend yourself against a skilled opponent.

Key Concepts

The interactive exercises of t'ai chi are built on four key concepts: stick, listen, neutralize, and redirect energy. They are best applied when the practitioner is mentally and physically relaxed, strongly but flexibly rooted, and accepts an aggressive force as opposed to resisting it.

When *sticking*, you learn to use your palm/forearm to intercept and adhere to an incoming arm or leg. The palms and fingers are the most sensitive parts of the body, and just as a blind person learns to "read" with his or her fingertips, a t'ai chi practitioner can learn to read body/mind movement in another person.

It may just be a coincidence that the palms and fingertips are said to have important "gates" in terms of ch'i flow and discharge. Whatever the reason, at high levels of skill you don't need to touch your partner or opponent physically but can stick to him with your mind/spirit.

Once stuck to your partner's limb or body, you use that physical or nonphysical contact to listen to the subtle and not-so-subtle muscle tremors that signal the beginning of an attack or change of direction. Such *listening* when (or, at high levels, *before*) a partner/opponent moves allows you a margin of error that you do not get if your tactics are based on physical reaction alone.

Unless you can stick and listen, you will be unable to *neutralize* force with the movement of your body/energy. This is not the use of muscle and leverage, although both of these are necessary participants in the process. Neutralizing is an erosion, a wearing away of the opponent's intention to strike as well as his physical momentum.

Neutralizing can be done even when you are being struck if you accept a force that makes contact with you and allow it to pass through your relaxed torso, down through the legs and feet, and into the ground. The analogy is that of turning yourself into a lightning rod for aggressive energy so that it is diverted and "grounded" into the earth and not allowed to vibrate harmfully inside you.

Redirecting a force involves leading it along a large or small elliptical or circular trajectory in the space around/between you and your partner, back to its point of origin. Redirecting can either be a relatively harmless return of the original energy in order to imbalance or frustrate your partner, or an intrusive acceleration. To do this you add your "ten ounces" (or more) of energy to what you've redirected.

At high levels of such skill, you can return the attacking energy to its source, even if it makes contact, so that it looks to an observer as if you have done nothing, even though the attacker is severely affected.

The physical aspects of such training can only be learned under the supervision of someone who knows how to do them. The physical tricks involved are simple, but only if your level of competence is already well-developed.

PUSH-HANDS

Push-hands is primarily concerned with the four actions found within Grasp Bird's Tail (ward-off, roll-back, press, push), and the two most frequently found forms of double push-hands either follow that sequence or reverse it.

Fixed-step practice teaches flexibility, rooting, and the use of the waist and torso. The moving practice (full-step, half-step, circling, cross-stepping) adds the dimensions of tempo and rhythm, as well as maintaining the proper space between you and your partner.

In most schools, you must achieve some competency in one of more of the traditional choreographed patterns of single push-hands before moving onto the more complex double push-hands patterns. The movements are done both from a fixed stance and with both partners moving their feet. Intermediate-level students can move onto free-style interaction using the patterns as a starting point for interplay.

Free-style push-hands can approach the speed and realism of sparring while still being relatively safe to practice. However, in the beginning it is important to practice all of the movements slowly and evenly until you have developed a feel for the interplay of physical tactics and the energy movement. The speed must be slow enough to allow the development of sensitivity but not so slow and lackadaisical that both partners are just going through the motions.

Unfortunately, in terms of personal development, many practitioners become fixated at the stage in which they achieve technical competence at the interplay of push-hands. Such competence easily brings complacency, and it is sad to see pairs of intermediate-level practitioners contentedly going through the motions of practice while discussing what they did the night before.

Tactically, the actions are complementary in that one leads smoothly to the next if the first fails. Thus, ward-off, if stopped by your partner, can be immediately changed to roll-back; if the latter fails, then press can explode from its ruins, etc.

In addition, each action can be foiled by another. Thus, an offensive use of ward-off can be neutralized by a defensive use of roll-back, and a defensive application of ward-off can be foiled by an offensive use of roll-back. It is important to remember that dividing actions into "offense" or "defense" is only useful for discussing theory and tactics.

While such changes are reflexive physical reactions learned through repetition, they are also, at the highest level, the product of a holistic maturity. Each action is a state of being and potential for change, not a finite set of criteria.

Practicing the interplay of the actions teaches you a great deal. However, you must be careful of your own joints as well as those of your partner when training. For example, when working at faster speeds and whipping your arms into position, be sure to use a little muscle tension throughout the movement. This is to prevent the arm from exceeding its natural range of motion.

You can easily give yourself "t'ai chi elbow" if you are too loose in your whipping action (in a misguided attempt to relax) and focus too sharply when the elbow has gone past its natural range of motion. Similarly, whipping actions can easily damage a wrist, elbow, or shoulder or cause whiplash to your partner's neck if you don't pay attention to the amount of energy you discharge and to how your partner reacts to it.

FOUR CORNERS

Da-lu (four corners) is also translated as "great pulling." This martial exercise emphasizes the tactical use of pull-down, split, elbow stroke, and shoulder stroke (and, in a few styles, slap) in an initially choreographed interaction.

Both practitioners move clockwise or counterclockwise while attacking and neutralizing each other's efforts. Only in t'ai chi and the internal arts can you find training tools built around such apparent contradictions as a square circle!

In some styles of da-lu, four corners refers to the four cardinal points (north, south, east, and west) to which you step while circling. In other styles, the name refers to the diagonal directions to which you step. Metaphorically, da-lu is a study of the total interplay of the eight cardinal trigrams of the *Chinese Book of Changes* (*I-Ching*).

On a simplistic level, it teaches you to deflect and redirect energy in a relaxed but potentially "explosive" manner that is relatively safe to practice with a partner. It also teaches both how to attack the joints of the arm and how to escape from such attacks.

Unfortunately, da-lu is an aspect of the interactive side of t'ai chi that is neglected in many schools. It is particularly valuable, as it can be used by relative beginners to explore movement safely and change within a choreographed format. More advanced students can move with more spirit and energy and begin doing spontaneous changes of direction, speed, and intensity—and relatively safely.

Da-lu makes excellent use of sticking and the related skills. However, some traditional patterns are obsessed with physical sticking with the hands and do not teach more advanced students how to "join with" and safely "let go" of a partner who varies his rhythm and intensity.

INTIMACY AND THE INTERACTIVE EXERCISES

There is a Zen fable which hints at the challenge of intimacy as experienced during push-hands.

An elderly monk and his apprentice were out walking when they reached a narrow and shallow stream that intersected their path. A young, attractive woman was hesitating on their side of the water. She was clearly reluctant to wade into the knee-deep water.

Without a word, the elderly monk swept the astonished woman into his arms and carried her the few feet across to the other side. His equally surprised apprentice hurried across behind them. The monk put the young woman down and she hurried off, obviously grateful, yet embarrassed by what had happened.

The monk continued along as if nothing had happened. His apprentice followed in respectful silence; however, after a few moments he was unable to restrain himself and said, "How could you touch a woman so intimately, master? We monks must be ever watchful of the lure of the world of the senses!"

The senior monk spoke without breaking stride: "I put her down on the other side of the water. Why are *you* still carrying her?"

He was still carrying her for the simple reason that intimacy, touching and being touched, is a basic human need. Physical contact is so important, especially if one has been deprived of it, that infants who lack nothing in institutional care except regular cuddling will frequently fail to develop normally and may even die.

Unfortunately, many individuals are deprived—for a variety of social, parental, and cultural reasons—of touching when they most need it, as children. They grow up being vaguely uneasy about physical contact unless it's clearly and appropriately of a sexual nature. Part of them wants physical closeness and part of them fears it because it has not been part of their experience.

Many North Americans suffer from such ambivalent feelings when it comes to intimacy, and nowhere is this more true than in the martial arts. Not all of us are capable of the maturity shown by the old monk. Part of the subconscious attraction of studying a martial art, especially one that allows a great deal of bodily contact (t'ai chi, jujutsu, wrestling, boxing, wing chun, etc.) is that it's "all right" to touch the others you're working with. However, because you're doing so in a regimented and physical manner, it is less threatening to yourself (and others, male or female) to do so.

Many people do push-hands that are rather stiff and overly choreographed. You're not likely to feel emotionally threatened by such practice (or learn anything of real value). Such persistent stiffness can be a psychological defense mechanism rather than a physical inability to relax.

The problem of intimacy in t'ai chi comes from the sensual slowness and sticky feel of doing some forms of push-hands and having to manipulate another person's body with your palms.

As we saw in a previous chapter, the Taoist theories of ch'i flow and the link between sexual energy and its cultivation have a great deal to do with t'ai chi-style energy. However, right now we're talking about emotional complications to the physical practice.

Some beginners fear intimacy so much (either because they're not used to it or because they have had traumatic experiences in the past) that they refuse to be touched or to make contact when doing so is necessary to learn the appropriate skills.

I have had partners start to shake, cry, and have anxiety attacks because of the feelings that suddenly overwhelmed them as a result of the contact of push-hands. Such feelings tend to surprise and embarrass both players and can cause those most affected to give up the use of such training practices.

By contrast to those who use their stiffness as a shield against intimacy, some people crave being touched and may consciously or subconsciously leave themselves open to contact when doing so is counterproductive in a learning or martial context.

Another problem lies simply in the differences between the male and female anatomy. If you're a man playing push-hands with a woman, where do you push? If you avoid the torso out of fear of accidental contact with breasts or lower abdomen, you're not doing yourself or your partner any favors. Neither of you will learn certain skills if one or both is unwilling to "play" without restriction.

At the same time, too much contact, accidental or otherwise, to the breasts can result in the tissue being pinched repeatedly. Such pain is not overly dangerous but is agonizing to women with large breasts and likely to discourage many from persevering.

Repeated contact may also embarrass one or both partners in a male-female pair into discarding such exercises for good or, conversely, turn the practice into some kind of martial foreplay!

This a real catch-22 proposition, which is only partly solved by a female player wearing chest protectors of some form or training only with other women. Neither is it a solution to exclude women from such training, as has been done in many schools since t'ai chi began.

This is not exclusively a cross-gender problem, either. During one of the first push-hand sessions I ever participated in, a male beginner was paired off with the male instructor. It was hot, and we were all wearing shorts. It soon became obvious to those watching that the novice was sexually aroused by the pushing practice. The instructor ended the practice abruptly, and we never saw that student in class again.

While the student in question may have been sexually excited because the instructor was male, it is also quite possible that he was just aroused by the physical contact. Being aroused through physical contact is part of human nature and is not necessarily gender-appropriate. The real answer to the question of intimacy in push-hands (or any martial training) is for each student to examine how he or she feels about the issue of physical contact with both men and women.

To really learn about yourself and others and to develop the necessary skills, you must accept that occasionally during push-hands you're going to feel either "turned on" or "turned off" by the contact or have that effect on your training partner.

On an ethical level, instructors must pay particular attention to not using such feelings to exploit their students. Some students already caught up in their feelings of respect/devotion to a teacher may be manipulated easily by the feelings aroused by push-hands practice into relationships that are of benefit only to the physical needs of the instructor. If you don't learn to accept (and ignore) such feelings, you may stop training or restrict its expression to the point where it may not be worth doing.

Do like the Zen monk: put being touched/aroused down when the moment is over and don't carry your emotional baggage from one training session to another.

CONCLUSION

The practice of the interactive side of this internal art can be very frustrating (and occasionally physically painful). For many North Americans, especially those who don't have a background in a martial art, the amount of physical contact can be frightening even in the most gentle and abstract forms of push-hands.

It is also threatening to put yourself into a situation in which you may not feel in control of the course of events. Sadly, those beginners who could most benefit from learning to accept a loss of face are those who are less likely to persevere in the interactive side of the art.

It is also very easy to fool yourself as to your level of competence. Someone talented solely at slow-motion uprooting forms of push-hands will succeed easily with those who have trained in the same methods but may fail dismally against someone who has trained in other approaches.

In some ways the most important push-hands lessons are truly learned by what the old masters called "investing in loss"—you learn best from situations in which you are apparently not being successful on a physical level.

In many ways, I have learned more about humility, relaxing, and putting tactics into perspective from being thrown repeatedly into a wall or gleefully pushed off-balance by a student than I have from successfully repeating what I already know.

In terms of martial exercise, you don't look for success as much as you look for your own deficiencies and how they can be improved with time and correct effort.

While the possibility of being robbed or assaulted is always present, it is also true that few of us will ever need self-defense skills or the ability to physically subdue and/or restrain someone.

Is there a reason, then, for the effort needed to learn and practice that side of t'ai chi as opposed to the solo form and/or the interactive martial exercises described in the previous chapter? Aside from the mental and physical benefits of such training, it provides an intangible insurance value which is there if you're unlucky enough to need it. Self-defense training also has that element of risky-play that appeals to many. However, its ultimate value lies in its use for *refining* your understanding of the art's subtle aspects.

If I have one problem with such training, it is that some instructors take it (and themselves) much too seriously. Learning self-defense because it's fun is as valid a factor as any—as long as the play is balanced with effort.

Sadly, many martial artists seem to forget their training when in a real

CHAPTER 7

T'AI CHI SELF-DEFENSE TRAINING PART ONE: CORE CONCEPTS

fight. I remember one instructor saying in all seriousness that he'd been attacked twice in twenty years of training/teaching time and that both times, he'd used a chair as an impromptu club against his attackers—effective tactics but hardly a technical expression of his art!

On the other hand, many internal stylists neglect to strive for a balance of mind and body and undertrain physically. The martial responses created by this kind of training tend to work best (if at all) with a fellow student.

While almost anyone can, with time, learn to defend himself, the challenge is to develop the potential to be able to do so successfully while doing it in an "internal" manner.

Applying t'ai chi ch'uan to a self-defense situation should imply a response that is appropriate and not based on blind reflex or the fears of the practitioner. Taoism urges that we find "the middle way," a balance between yin and yang, between submission and aggressiveness.

Such skills should preserve your *physical* integrity or that of an innocent party, but not necessarily your emotional integrity, as that can only be harmed if you allow it. If such skills are used appropriately, then I see no need to reconcile the life-enhancing aims of t'ai chi with the rare need for combat.

The phrase that advocates the ethical superiority of "turning the other cheek" has been interpreted as meaning that you should accept abuse even to the extent of inviting more on the other side in order to restore peace. However, such an interpretation is more likely to incite an escalation of aggression. A little common sense would suggest that an attacker who could easily be stopped from further violence by a demonstration of nonaggression would not likely be attacking in the first place.

"Turning the other cheek" should be more realistically interpreted as moving with the force of an attack as it hits so that you absorb some, if not all, of the impact. You then have the choice of ignoring the attack or returning it.

In addition, this attitude is best applied in situations in which tempers have been lost temporarily and a blow is struck out of frustration or passion. Such cases often involve family, workmates, friends, or acquaintances, and not retaliating is likely the best way to prevent the escalation of violence. When I say not retaliating, I mean not hitting back; this does not imply that you must refrain from parrying or avoiding the blows directed at you.

Turning the other cheek is a fine moral principle on a symbolic level and one that t'ai chi demonstrates both on a philosophical and practical level, but it should not become a rationalization for accepting abuse. Approached this way, self-defense becomes an extension of maintaining one aspect of physical health (yes, I'm rationalizing violence, but life sometimes demands that this be done).

Unfortunately, the majority of North American instructors are still mainly oriented to form and other solo exercises like ch'i-kung. Schools that practice competent uprooting, push-hands, and da-lu are hard to find, and those that emphasize more relevant self-defense tactics are even more rare. Sadly, teachers like Erle Montaigue, Liang Shou-Yu, William C.C. Chen, and Dr. Yang Jwing Ming are rare martial "treasures." However, the effort needed to train with such instructors, even in the form of short-term seminars far from home, is justified in terms of the potential benefits for the serious student.

BASIC SELF-DEFENSE TRAINING

A basic self-defense program includes the entire spectrum of solo form work combined with those tactics and training methods complementary to the skills of sticking, listening, neutralizing, and redirecting, as developed through tui shou, da-lu, and other sensitivity exercises.

Posture Applications

The first stage of learning valid self-defense skills through t'ai chi involves practicing the individual postures as defensive moves against controlled but determined attacks. This can be done randomly or in a choreographed sequence—the latter is taught as a variety of traditional two-person exercises or application forms in some styles of t'ai chi.

Long or complicated two-person forms are useful in that you and your partner can attack and defend with spirit, as both of you know what is coming next. Such choreography means that you don't have to worry unduly about your partner being surprised by a spontaneous move and unable to cope with a tactic. However, when a pair of partners are roughly equal in skill and experience, such two-person forms can also easily become performance arts that bring a false sense of security in terms of developing skills that could be used effectively against a *spontaneous* and *determined* attack.

My opinion is that you should devote the bulk of your training time to individual postures and varied applications. Each of the traditional postures has a variety of tactical functions, depending on your level of competence as well as the size of your partner and the angle and type of attack. A study of the function of the form's postures provides a basic training for learning how to deal with attacks that come out of nowhere.

Real assaults are—unlike in the movies and sporting events where the contestants are young, well-trained, and conditioned—short, nasty, and largely unprovoked. Similarly, unless your attacker is a rank amateur, he or she is not going to let you have a limb to stick to initially.

If you cannot bridge the space separating you from your attacker as well as he can, you're left in a poor tactical position. Unfortunately, such skills are almost impossible to learn from a strict adherence to traditional push-hands and da-lu, as these are usually begun with the two partners already in contact.

In addition, the student who does not practice and gain at least some skill in techniques using both sides of the body will be at a severe disadvantage against a more ambidextrous opponent or, even worse, against someone whose dominant (stronger) side is opposite his or hers.

My own feeling is that the best way to train is to emphasize skill enhancement on your dominant side and develop selected skills on the weaker side to use as an element of surprise.

The main tactical tools of the t'ai chi practitioner are the arms/hands—the leg techniques are not as obvious or predominant as in many fighting systems.

In the modern Yang forms, there are only three kicks: Separate and Kick with the Foot, Separate and Kick with the

Heel, and Lotus Kick. The first is a sweep upward with the top or ball of the foot into the opponent's crotch, the second is a strike with the heel into the bladder area to cause internal injuries, and the third is used to set up a sweep of your opponent's leg or to strike with a clockwise sweep into the kidney area.

In t'ai chi, the feet and legs are used to provide a strong, stable, and mobile platform for the upper body, which is used offensively and defensively. Especially in terms of self-defense, the legs should only be used as a "secret" weapon if your arms and hands are immobilized or if your opponent is off balance or a poor fighter.

That said, it is also true that the feet and knees can be used effectively to trip and/or sweep an opponent's legs through increasing leverage when working in close while simultaneously applying energy with the arms.

For example, if I use press on an opponent diagonally across his or her center of gravity, he will feel a concussion or be pushed away (depending on the type of press being used). However, if I use the same tactic from a close range while sticking with my lead foot to the side or behind his lead foot—the effect of my technique will be greatly enhanced.

The "Heart" Factor

Having heart (courage in Western terms) is a little-talked-about aspect of self-defense training, but a crucial one. Unfortunately, many people are first drawn to the martial arts by fear—fear of being embarrassed, harassed, assaulted, or revictimized. Overcoming such fears is part of the process of maturing both as an individual and a martial artist.

As a beginner, the first step to understanding fear is going to a t'ai chi class for the first time and submitting yourself to new people and new experiences. Achieving an intermediate level of skill and teaching much stronger or bigger students who want proof that your skills are valid is a second step. Becoming an instructor and demonstrating to indifferent or possibly hostile spectators is a third step. Being required to use your skills against a real aggressor, no matter what your level, is the final step.

On a traditional level, the Chinese feel the heart to be the center for the fighting spirit, and that was partly why the heart was such a frequent target in hard and soft kung-fu styles. Aside from its physical vulnerability, damaging the heart was seen as literally robbing an opponent of his will to fight.

The aim of putting heart in your tactics is *not* to create a response dominated by an emotion such as fear or excitement. The adrenaline energy produced by fear is exhausted quickly.

For example, during the European Dark Ages, Viking *berserkers* (who gave us the English word for a wild and frenzied attack) would enter autohypnotic trances in which they "became" bears or wolves, gaining immunity to pain and minor injuries while intensifying the savagery of their onslaught. Such intensity was, not surprisingly, difficult for a poorly trained feudal militia to face. However, disciplined troops were often able to endure the ferocity of the initial assault, knowing that such rage was impossible to sustain.

Similarly, the "hot" fighter may well succeed with an initial onslaught on an amateur but be unable to overcome a more disciplined opponent who channels his emotions and uses that energy as *part*, not the *whole*, of a tactical effort.

Courage is, on a basic level, the willingness to persevere despite being afraid. True courage is not a denial of fear but an acceptance of it and the willingness (the heart) to continue despite that fear.

On an emotional level, this also means accepting that you find pleasure in martial training. This acceptance allows you to channel such emotional energies in a martial (and moral) fashion as opposed to feeling guilty over enjoying the contact and the combative play.

Don't Get Hit!

The t'ai chi approach to self-defense in terms of accepting and redirecting oncoming force implies that you keep from being hit. Ideally, you do so without any desire to harm your aggressor and without any preconceived course of reaction to the attack. In theory, your attacker will become discouraged by a lack of success or exhaust himself and cease attacking without either of you being hurt.

As an example, like the "entering" (irimi) of aikido, which is the basis of allowing the attacker to throw himself, the famous Grasp Bird's Tail sequence of t'ai chi allows the defender to stick to an oncoming force until the attacker persists in blocking his own actions or bouncing himself away. At the highest (and rarest) level of understanding, such skill goes beyond self-defense and becomes an inner calm and physical response which not only refuses to contend but is beyond concepts like fighting and refraining from fighting.

Attack as You Defend!

If, like me, your skill and emotional maturity don't guarantee that you can live up to such lofty levels, I recommend the t'ai chi tactic of attacking as you defend.

As a martial art, t'ai chi is difficult to learn because it demands the ability to start after your opponent but still get there first in terms of redirecting his or her energy while adding your own "ten ounces" to it.

Unfortunately, anxiety over doing things correctly, especially when it affects one's ability to stop aggression, often leads to trying to guess what the other person's moves will be. Trying to second guess an opponent's moves will play into the hands (and feet) of an experienced brawler or sophisticated fighter who can change his rhythm and intensity as necessary.

While it seems aggressive, this is a lesser manifestation of not getting hit. By causing pain or inflicting a justifiable amount of damage as you neutralize an attack, you increase your own margin of safety by encouraging the attacker to decide—immediately—that he's better off going elsewhere with his aggression.

Don't Get Hit First!

If you can't avoid being struck (and it happens unless your skills are exceptional), make sure you achieve contact as or, better still, *before* the aggressor's strike sinks in. Keep in mind the t'ai chi axiom, "starting after your opponent but reaching him first." By striking even marginally before he does, you will, at the least, rob his attack of some impact and, at best, stop it completely.

It is also important to remember that the first strike of any real fight is often the deciding factor in survival. Whoever is

struck first may well be put on the defensive psychologically—
quite different from being a tactical defensive fighter. In addition, being hit first may finish you due to the impact and/or the
target affected.

According to some sources, one of the most famous practitioners of kali, a Filipino martial art, was a blind woman
whose ability to sense and stick to an attack was such that
she was untouchable. Remember that their fights were with
hardwood sticks or edged weapons and brutally short-lived—
they ended almost immediately with one person dead,
maimed, or incapacitated.

A highly sensitive individual, even a blind one, who can stick
to the *first* strike, redirect it, and simultaneously counterattack
effectively will most likely be the one to survive.

It Doesn't Matter if You're Hit!

Absorbing, redirecting, and discharging energy are most easily done when using a hand or forearm to stick with and lead the
opponent's power where you want it. However, at a higher level
you stick with whatever part of your body is struck and use it, not
the hand/arm, to neutralize whatever force is thrown your way.

Whatever the real reasons (mind over matter, training the
ch'i), such skills can minimize the power of strikes to all but
the most important acupuncture points and parts of the body:
eyes, front of the throat, cranial hinge, and testicles being the
most obvious exceptions. For those experienced in contact
sparring, the hormonal rush caused by the fight-or-flight syndrome will negate the pain and trauma caused by all but the
most effective blows.

Neutralizing a hit bears some relation to the apparent insensi-
bility of the brawler who wades in, ignoring the pain, until he
scores or is hit somewhere vital. Such brawling does illustrate the
use (or absence) of mind in absorbing and ignoring pain that
would stop someone who fears pain and is not used to being hit.

Feeling pain is the mind/body's trigger for removing yourself from
a danger before the damage is too great. Ignoring pain can be stupid
in the sense that you may be damaged beyond biological repair.

However, the untrained individual usually overreacts to even the suggestion of pain (i.e., the fear of the event) and tries to compensate for that fear by undertraining or being overly cautious. Proper training teaches that pain can often be *safely* ignored and that being struck, when you move with and/or sink the attacking energy, no longer hurts—in part, because you no longer fear being hurt. Accepting and internalizing this on a gut level is one of the most difficult t'ai chi skills to develop. In some ways it is also the most important.

Being used to getting hit is what makes the average bar brawler, boxer, or kickboxer (no matter what the style) effective in a way that most t'ai chi practitioners *of any level of expertise* cannot hope to match. How you react to being hit (relaxed or tense, fearful or calm) and how you return that aggressive force are the yin/yang of t'ai chi self-defense.

Unfortunately, these are difficult skills to develop safely, as it is easy for injuries to occur, especially when beginners work with each other. It is also easy for such training to degenerate into a reliance on "skillful forcing."

To Stick or Not to Stick

Learning to stick is an essential tool of t'ai chi combat as long as it is done properly and *not* as a blind response. You don't use a wrench to hammer in a nail just because you're accustomed to the feel of the former and it's immediately at hand. You use the tool best suited to the task at hand. Doing otherwise is the mark of an amateur and is likely to result in injury!

The classical skills of t'ai chi—sticking, listening, neutralizing, and redirecting—are essential but must never be done as a blind response to physical stimuli. After learning such skills, one must learn when and how *not to* apply them for a martial purpose.

T'ai chi is a defensive, reactive art, and this has definite ethical and tactical advantages. However, paradoxically, this very strength can be a disadvantage in that you cannot survive a prolonged attack by a superior force through a static, passive defense—no matter how well-rooted. (For example, the Great Wall of China never stopped a determined invader, only the amateurs.)

A good punch is a good punch. Any soft stylist who has spent most of his training doing form and feels an intellectual contempt for the lack of sophistication of a blow from a hard stylist will also probably feel a great deal of pain if he has one thrown his way. Being "sticky" and being able to defend yourself are not automatically synonymous!

In addition, sticking skills can be a liability if you have little experience working with someone who is trying to get you to stick t ohis arm for his own ends. For example, one of my favorite tactics to close the distance between myself and a student when sparring is to suddenly thrust a hand within his reach. If he unthinkingly sticks to it without simultaneously initiating a counterattack, I simply use his hand to drag him off balance and into range.

It is important to remember that most of the founding fathers of t'ai chi had extensive and varied backgrounds in the martial arts before they got into t'ai chi. They developed push-hands and other sensitivity exercises as means of *refining* their combat skills.

Unfortunately, doing such exercises without previous or realistic combat skills means that you're refining without having the necessary raw materials.

Personal Space, Rhythm, Speed, and Timing

One of the hardest concepts to understand in terms of self-defense is that of defining and maintaining a personal space. This space is a mental "cushion" about a foot wide which covers you like a thick, invisible covering. On a physical level, you must learn to ignore any movement by an opponent that doesn't intrude into your personal space.

If you overreact to tentative body movements by an opponent, he may well succeed in faking an initial move that lures you into moving prematurely or creating openings for a sudden determined attack. If you stand there passively or overroot yourself, you risk him being able to insert his hands or feet through the personal space easily and make contact with your body.

If your skill levels are high, his making contact doesn't matter as much. If they aren't . . .

The idea is to relax as much as possible while remaining intent on *his* intent. You should either move constantly on the spot (like a good boxer) or be completely still until you're sure that a movement toward you is fully committed and not just a feint.

At a higher level, one not easy to do consistently, personal space becomes an invisible extension of your body—a ch'i safety zone—and committed intrusions into that space are sensed by your spirit, not by your eyes or palms or forearms.

When moving with, as opposed to reacting to, an opponent, the rhythms we produce are a microcosmic replica of those of existence. As in Taoist thought, modern quantum physics now suggests that movement and rhythm are essential properties of existence and that all matter, whether living or inert, is involved in a continuous cosmic dance. The universal appeal of music and dance, especially with beats that mimic the heartbeat, should tell us how important rhythm is to the human spirit.

To understand movement and its relationship to combat, you must learn to understand how it affects your body by practicing at a variety of speeds, learning to create your own rhythms and maintain them while your opponent is trying to disrupt them. With time and experience you will learn to intrude your own rhythms on the personal space of those you practice with, to their martial detriment.

Interestingly enough, doing applications (as well as form) slowly and evenly is not as ineffective, in martial terms, as it would first appear. Police officers who have survived one-on-one gun duels at close range almost all speak of having experienced a "slowing down" of time while focused on surviving a potentially lethal attack. They report that the events seemed to take place in a dreamlike slow motion.

When you consider that t'ai chi was designed as a method of self-defense, it is interesting to speculate on whether or not any of its founding fathers ever had such experiences in combat and decided to mimic it through form practice.

It is more obviously true that, initially, working slowly is the best way to refine and internalize the motor skills necessary for any physical activity.

It is equally true that speed is also an essential aspect of understanding rhythm. To truly get an appreciation of this, it is essential that you put on protective gear occasionally and practice tactics with some degree of contact to the body. Alternatively, striking a heavy bag or makiwara while shadow boxing is another way to explore rhythm and its variations when force (internal or otherwise) is involved.

Fa-ch'ing

An internal discharge of energy strike (fa-ch'ing) is, like most of t'ai chi, both an easy and difficult tactic to develop in terms of doing it spontaneously and correctly. It is also difficult to practice safely on a fellow student.

Similar, but not identical, to Bruce Lee's famous "one-inch punch," such short-range power has to be experienced to be believed.

Leaving aside the concepts of ch'i flow for a moment, you can think of fa-ch'ing in this way: the human body is composed mainly of water, and, by means of correct alignment and relaxation, you learn to strike it with a concussive, rather than blunt, impact. The effect is like that of an explosion in the water.

Fishing with dynamite is illegal in most countries because the shock waves of even a small explosion kill more fish, at greater distances from the source of the blast, than can be harvested for responsible use. Similarly, short power can be imagined as creating a hydrostatic shock wave in the target. In addition, if the person hit is stiff, that stiffness just magnifies the effect of the tremors for destructive purposes.

Erle Montaigue calls fa-ch'ing a "sneeze" reflex that involves the whole body; William C.C. Chen has referred to such power as "waking-up," as when you respond with a powerful jerk of the torso and limbs if startled out of a light sleep.

I like to describe it as the energy of a whip which travels in a wave along its length, to be discharged with explosive force at the tip. The base of the spine/abdomen (lower tan tien) becomes the handle of the whip, the spine and arm(s) its length, and the palm and fingers the tip which discharges the strike. The mind/spirit is the invisible hand holding and cracking the whip.

You can also think of a fa-ch'ing strike as an invisible grenade that you thrust *into* the target: as you remove your hand, the safety pin is released, and the explosion takes place *inside* the target, not on the surface of the skin.

Training such strikes in the air can teach you how to discharge energy with speed but can also lead to elbow and shoulder strain if you don't do it correctly. However, training in the air can't teach you how to allow your joints to absorb the stress of hitting something solid/yielding without also absorbing all of your energy before it can enter the target.

To develop optimal skills, you must practice striking in the air, on a variety of hard and yielding inanimate surfaces, and on another person. I have observed that beginners tend to hurt the wrist and/or elbows in learning how to strike properly because they have no experience hitting anything solid. However, those used to hitting a heavy bag may not have much actual penetration power to their strikes initially because the human body can yield more effectively than a heavy bag.

There's been quite a controversy among martial artists in recent years over the importance of size and strength. Generally speaking, those involved in the hard styles seem to feel that the bigger and stronger you are, the better it is for your potential fighting ability.

Conversely, those training in the internal styles are as likely to feel that size and strength play a lesser role.

Which camp is correct? They can't both be, or can they? The answer for the t'ai chi player, unfortunately for those who like their answers black *or* white, is both yes and no.

Each variation of physique (tall, short, heavy, light, long-reach, short-reach) can have advantages as long as you pay strict attention to the combative principles of t'ai chi and make your partner or opponent obey your rules.

For example, a tall individual can use a long arm reach to great effect against a shorter opponent. However, he or she can lose that advantage if the smaller person can get in close and stick effectively to disrupt the tall person's lines of

CHAPTER 8

T'AI CHI SELF-DEFENSE TRAINING PART TWO: MAXIMIZING YOUR TRAINING

attack and sense of balance. The shorter person can then use the great stability of his or her lower center of gravity to apply energy in an upward direction.

Conversely, a short individual can make effective use of a lower center of gravity against a taller opponent but only by refraining from accidentally pulling the larger mass into him so that the bigger person can use "down" energy to crushing effect.

Having just implied that all factors are relative, it is also true that being big and/or strong is often an important, even decisive, factor. The larger individual will have the edge if all other factors (skill, experience, heart) are equal.

Fortunately for those of smaller size, such factors are rarely equal. Consequently, it is just as true that a small individual will be able to successfully train with much larger/stronger individuals who have less skill or experience. The smaller person of high skill will also be able to succeed combatively against bigger assailants.

Conversely, this does not apply to sport competitions where rules and factors of safety limit the use of those tactics that are most effective in self-defense. Consequently, t'ai chi competitions (like boxing, wrestling, etc.) divide their participants into weight classes.

However, leaving competition aside, smaller students must pay strict attention to applying the principles of t'ai chi, as those half-hearted applications which work on an inexperienced classmate of the same mass will probably fail miserably on a larger individual with roughly the same level of skill.

On the other hand, it is easier for smaller-sized students to know that they are training properly and applying the t'ai chi principles properly when they train with someone larger. If their tactics work, then they know that their success is most likely based on the correct use of t'ai chi principles.

A larger individual can cheat without even knowing he or she is doing so by using mass or strength to supplement a partial use of the principles. Thus, it becomes just as essential for larger students to pay particular attention to using principles and not just mass.

On a tactical level, it is essential that you not allow a hand or forearm to be grabbed and immobilized, *even for a moment*, especially if the attacker is considerably bigger. Being large, I have noted that many of my lighter students and those of other styles with whom I've worked have difficulty dealing with such tactics.

That's why releasing, bouncing, and folding techniques are so essential to the repertoire of a t'ai chi player. If you allow a hand or arm to be held (and I'm not necessarily talking about joint-locking of any kind), you limit your ability to use the waist or move your feet. When this happens, you can't as easily use the total effort which is (or should be) a characteristic of t'ai chi.

Internal arts players who are just beginning to get in touch with their ability to receive and discharge energy must also be very careful when practicing with a partner so that the latter doesn't end up with internal injuries or bone fractures through an unexpected application of the principles.

The larger beginner may not realize just how effective mass/strength can be against a smaller partner when the principles are added to those factors. Similarly, the smaller student may neglect to restrain himself in applying the principles against a larger partner because he doesn't realize just how awesome the effect can be on a stiff opponent—no matter what his or her relative mass.

In some ways, the true test of t'ai chi competence isn't obtaining the energy use so much as learning to use it judiciously on a spontaneous level.

With a little aptitude and proper instruction, most t'ai chi players, no matter what their relative size, can learn to discharge t'ai chi-style energy before they are ready to do so *safely* for themselves and their partners. However, this does not mean that mass/weight of a partner/opponent is a negligible factor. If your instructor tells you the opposite, he is either exceptionally skilled or just lucky that no one big and talented has seen fit to confront him!

Visualization

Modern research into the use of the imagination has shown that the founding fathers of t'ai chi were on the right track in terms of suggesting the value of mentally "fighting" with an opponent. Doing this while practicing solo form or applications training is an effective means of enhancing the physical performance of such skills. Mental imagery combined with physical practice provides the quickest route to improvement.

Research by North American and Eastern European sports scientists has shown that using "creative visualization," as it is sometimes called, has a beneficial effect on individual performance. The key word here is *individual*.

By imagining myself throwing a better punch or deflecting a kick with greater skill, I can actually improve my mechanical performance of those techniques through the use of the mind. However, the basic skills must already be stored in the mind and body before they can be improved. In addition, no matter how vivid my imagination, I cannot mentally anticipate the changes and rapid-fire tactics of a real opponent. Such visualization may bring a false sense of security. Such mind games are called "useless effort" (yu-wei).

Relaxing, redirecting, and applying energy while under pressure are best learned through training with others, as factors such as an opponent's size, strength, and skill can only be understood through interacting with a variety of partners (or, if you want to do it the hard way, opponents). However, once you have developed a physical understanding of working with a partner, you can begin to use visualization while doing form or before practicing with a partner to refine the quality of both the form and of your martial function. At this point, physical practice is less necessary than it once was.

Conversely, if you visualize all the time you risk becoming obsessed with martial function. During at least some of your form practice, you should also be experiencing "inner quiet" for the health benefits that such a state can bring.

The Use of Sound

Biologically, we seem genetically programmed to startle and prepare for flight at sudden loud noises—a survival mechanism present in animals. For example, the feelings evoked by bagpipes, originally weapons of war, make it easy to understand how such sounds on a battlefield would either inspire or demoralize (especially, in the latter case, when heard for the first time).

Martial cries or sounds can provide a tactical advantage if you momentarily throw an opponent off balance with a sudden cry. A few traditionalists would also argue that specific sounds, when done by an expert, can either heal or harm the listener.

This sounds far-fetched until we consider how a talented singer can shatter glass with the power of his or her voice. In addition, studies on the effects of sound waves have shown that some frequencies actually cause physical damage and/or even temporary paralysis to the nervous system.

However, to be most effective, such vibrations of air particles must come from deep within the user. Such energy production is difficult, as it must be both deliberate and spontaneous.

In his book *Zen and the Art of Archery*, Eugene Herrigel, the aged master of the Japanese bow, emphasizes that the archer must not feel himself separate from the bow/arrow and the process of firing. There is no mental decision to fire the arrow. When the moment is right, the arrow and string simply part company.

In that classic movie *The Seven Samurai*, the climatic battle scene takes place in the gloom and mud of a raging rainstorm. The leader of the *ronin* is shown braced against the wind and rain as he pulls his bow to shoot the advancing bandits out of the saddle as they attack.

The old samurai—even though drenched and exhausted—has the most serene look of concentration as he draws and holds the bow before firing. Despite the weather and the battle raging around him, the arrows that he fires in rapid succession seem to leave the bow of their own accord.

Similarly, a shout comes not just because you want to tighten your abdomen, aid in expelling the breath/chi, or frighten/harm your opponent, but because it is "right" to yell. Such a shout is an indication of proper breathing, but it is also an indication of true spontaneity.

Such a cry becomes an expression of unity and self, not just a scream of fear or an attempt to intimidate. In this sense, you cannot train to improve such a cry; it comes from the tan tien, at the right moment, or not at all.

Some teachers of t'ai chi advocate the use of certain audible sounds to accompany the intake and expelling of the breath (the "hen" and "ha" sounds). Such training has merit as long as the practitioner does not get into the habit of grunting "ha" as a matter of accompaniment to every technique!

Tactically, such cries are best used once—the first time—against an experienced fighter. There is also an old Chinese expression about the relationship between martial yells and combat skill that translates as, "The fiercest dog bites without barking a warning!"

Manipulating the Joints

Chin-n'a (joint-locking, twisting, or striking) can be a very effective tactic, especially if you are already in contact with an opponent and suddenly find yourself in a position of advantage in relation to the joint(s).

It is also important to remember that there are a great variety of joints in the human body—not just in the limbs. The shoulders, hips, spinal vertebrae, and the junctions where the ribs connect to the sternum and spine are all valuable targets, if you have trained to attack them. Similarly, you have to know how to defend such vulnerable areas.

You are unlikely to be attacked by a well-trained fighter who specializes in such targets. However, you should always train to counter the difficult attacks as well as the easy ones. Otherwise "Murphy's Law" (whatever can go wrong . . . will!) may well ensure that the only assault you ever face will be your last!

Hands Strum the Lute, High Pat the Horse, and Slanting Flying are all examples of t'ai chi postures that strike the nerves/meridians/joints to cause pain and structural damage, and use leverage to destroy balance in an opponent. However, catching a joint to immobilize it is a different matter. The martial arts movies, as well as some instructors, would have us believe that you can snap an elbow when the arm in question is in midflight or catch a moving leg to immobilize it with relative ease.

Someone of exceptional skill and martial experience may be able to do so safely, but don't try it against a hardened streetfighter after one or two years of half-hearted training. A good kick or jab can be redirected or retracted with alarming speed. You can hardly stick to something you can't even see (unless your skills are exceptional—few t'ai chi instructors, much less their students, have such martial sensitivity).

It is a well-known axiom in the martial arts that the best defense against someone who grapples you is to strike him while he is beginning to apply his technique.

If you cannot adversely affect someone's balance and/or hurt him or her immediately to provide a distraction for your follow-up grappling, don't try to do it. In addition, if you're much lighter or smaller, then it is usually too risky to come into grappling range voluntarily. However, even if you can't catch a fast jab, you may still be able to numb the arm or damage a joint while neutralizing or parrying the attack. You should not ignore the relative kindness of crippling a joint as opposed to blinding or killing someone who has tried to assault you, especially if weapons are involved.

MAXIMIZING YOUR SELF-DEFENSE TRAINING

Two questions should be uppermost in the minds of any instructor or student in regard to self-defense training: is it safe, and is it realistic?

Like any seemingly contradictory aspect of training, these two do not necessarily have to be mutually exclusive—but often they are.

To make your training in posture applications, push-hands, da-lu, or san shou (whether you translate san shou as free-style push-hands or as an application form) effective, you need a variety of partners you can trust—to work *both* of you as hard as possible while doing so as safely as possible.

One way to maximize the use of a good sparring partner is using safety gear. Like doing form as well as martial function in t'ai chi, combining a sparring partner with safety gear gives you a return on your investment of time and effort that is greater than the sum of the individual parts.

Safety Gear

Protective padding/safety equipment can provide the opportunity to train with more of a combat edge without greatly increasing the risk of injury. However, the use of such equipment can also create its own set of problems.

Psychologically, the use of such gear, especially by relative beginners, induces fear of contact because the training suddenly seems more serious when such equipment is worn. This fear may cause some to stop training of any kind and cause others to toss sensitivity, yielding, and centering aside in favor of brute strength and crude technique.

Instead of pairs of students training a little more energetically because of the safety factor allowed by such gear, you're as likely to end up with students who circle each other too cautiously or who batter fiercely at each other because of the presumption that protective gear has suddenly made them invulnerable.

This is particularly crucial when learning unarmed tactics against knives and clubs, even wooden or rubber ones. A hard plastic knife point will blind you as readily as metal if thrust into your eye! It can be easy to forget that wooden weapons can maim and that plastic and padding don't have the same "stopping" value as metal or leather armor.

You must also come to terms with the problem that has troubled fighters for thousands of years: if the protective gear is to be truly effective, it limits mobility and peripheral vision; if light enough not to limit those factors, it provides less protection.

For unarmed self-defense practice, the minimal equipment includes good headgear, a throat guard, eye-protectors, a chest piece, an athletic cup, and shin guards. If you wear forearm/fist protectors and/or padded gloves, you must sacrifice a great deal of the feeling that makes t'ai chi tactics so effective.

For self-defense applications against weapons, you need the above as well as a solid helmet and face mask, shoulder/upper-arm pads, a heavy-duty throat guard, and padded gloves with fingers. Hard shin and knee pads are also useful, as are upper-thigh protectors.

Purchasing safety gear designed for martial arts usage is an expensive option if you must purchase by mail and/or from other countries. My students and I use padding designed for a variety of more mundane contact sports. Such equipment is more readily available than that designed for martial arts use, is cheaper, and gives you the option of looking like an extra from that Mel Gibson epic, *Road Warrior*.

The use of protective gear allows for moderate or heavy contact to the *body* for at least part of your training and gets you (and your partner) used to making contact with force and *with being hit*. You can't learn how to absorb, redirect, or (at its crudest) ignore being hit unless you actually get hit!

However, for the average practitioner of self-defense skills, there is no need for training with hard, deliberate contact to the leg joints (as is popular in Thai boxing) or to the head. Protective headgear should be worn to minimize the chance of injury from *accidental* contact.

Repeated contact to the head destroys brain cells and can cause mental/physical deterioration. T'ai chi skills are meant as much to improve and maintain health as they are to give you self-defense skills.

Sparring Partner

A good training/sparring partner is difficult to find and, as with any relationship, difficult to keep. Both partners must learn and grow from the training, or one will surely grow tired of being a human "punching bag" at some point.

You must also take care that the need to grow and evolve in your skills doesn't just become a competition between you and your partner(s) to see who will become the best. Being the best is a meaningless concept, because there is always someone somewhere who does what you are doing better. This is also the reason for training with a variety of partners so that you have exposure to a variety of personalities, physical types, and ranges of skill. What works with the thirty-year-old you've been training with regularly for a year may well fail miserably with a younger, street-wise opponent.

A good sparring/training partner is essential to martial development. In fact, one of the best selfish reasons for teaching t'ai chi or any other martial art is having the opportunity to train regularly with people who share your interest and want to evolve along similar paths.

While Thai boxers make most modern t'ai chi practitioners seem ineffective as fighters, even such comparatively moderate training as I have just advocated may seem antithetical to the soft aspects of the art. Perhaps I and those who share my attitudes are a little too martial for our own good; however, you can't, as the saying goes, "cook eggs without breaking some shells."

Any instructor who tells you that you can learn self-defense without some contact, even if accidental, is at best self-deceiving; at worst a liar.

DEFENDING AGAINST MULTIPLE ATTACKERS

The use of safety gear also permits you to explore training against more than one attacker at a time. The use of such gear is essential *for the attackers*, not the student defending. The latter is likely to overreact at first and use more muscle or fa-ch'ing than is necessary or safe.

The individual tactics of dealing with two or more attackers simultaneously can only be dealt with under the supervision of an instructor. However, in theoretical terms, numbers don't count as much as skill and spirit on the part of a solitary defender.

Amateurs use the intimidation of numbers as a tactic and are likely to get in each other's way if they try to attack you simultaneously. This becomes dangerous only if one can immobilize you while the others concentrate on causing damage.

In addition, alcohol, drugs, and group dynamics create a tension that feeds on itself: the dominant male of the group seeks to reinforce that superiority while the others seek to prove their worth to the leader and to each other.

A strategic withdrawal ("running like hell," if that is safely possible) or an immediate attack on your part is almost always necessary when dealing with more than one opponent. Attacking an obvious leader or the largest individual first and beating him will give you a small but important psychological edge.

Discouraging the hostility or aggression of a stranger with a show of skill may well encourage him or her to stop being physically annoying. However, when he has friends/supporters present, such half-measures will probably only embarrass him into further violence.

In addition, when your attackers have been taking drugs or drinking they are much less susceptible to psychological intimidation and to being warned off by superficial pain. In such a situation, you may have to attempt to incapacitate them by attacking vital points (e.g., the knee to prevent further mobility).

It is particularly essential when working against more than one attacker that you not lose your balance, even momentarily, or use tactics that might pull one attacker onto you (even if you've badly injured him in the process). While you're reeling from their slamming into you or trying to support their dead weight, the others will find it much easier to harm you.

Being knocked down is particularly dangerous when defending against multiple attackers, as they can easily keep you from getting up by surrounding you. Once you're on the ground and encircled, it's too late. If you relax properly while being kicked, you *may* survive by tucking your knees up to protect your abdomen/genitals and cradling your neck and head in your arms.

In some ways, an experienced pair of attackers is more dangerous than three or four amateurs, especially if the two are used to working as a tactical team and not as individuals. Fortunately for the average student of self-defense, such professionals are few and far between.

Unarmed Defense against Weapons

Sadly, the open and concealed carrying of knives has increased dramatically in the last few years. In terms of blunt impact weapons, tire irons, baseball bats, and pieces of pipe are frequent "improvised" weapons.

Fortunately, real expertise with either an edged weapon or club usually centers around martial arts training, and such training tends to make the practitioner less violent rather than more so. However, while it is comparatively rare to encounter a well-trained attacker, it is no longer rare to be faced by some street tough who has had some training, either in a legitimate club or in prison (not all occupational training in such institutions is rehabilitating!).

Parents like to tell their children, "Don't play with knives; you're going to get cut!" This also applies to adults forced to play with knives. Unlike in the movies, a knife fight is usually over almost as soon as it begins, with one or both participants injured.

It's how you react to being cut and the severity and type of injury that you inflict or endure that will make the ultimate difference to your survival. Despite this, you can't afford to take chances with such wounds. Deep stab wounds in particular can cause clinical shock almost instantly, which, by itself, can kill.

Blows to the head can easily cause unconsciousness, severe brain damage, or death.

Slashes are more psychologically threatening initially than they are physically (unless the eyes or major arteries, surprisingly difficult targets, are cut), as they are rarely deep, but they can cause heavy bleeding.

Many people panic at the first sign of blood, especially their own. Such emotion may so distract you that your attacker uses your confusion to find an opening for a lethal follow-up blow.

Similarly, panic may make you try to block or grab a knife automatically to prevent further damage. Doing so will only get your hands slashed and prevent you from using them effectively. If cut superficially, you must allow adrenaline stimulated by the infamous "flight-or-fight" syndrome to mask the extent of your injuries until you can seek medical attention safely.

The only tactical difference between knives and clubs is that you may be able to ignore being hit with a club, depending on where you are struck and your skill/strength. In addition, you may be able to grab a club after slowing down or stopping its trajectory or hurting its wielder; you can never do that with an edged weapon.

If you can't retreat from an attack safely, watch the opponent but don't stare at the weapon, as a good fighter will try to mesmerize you with it so that he can kick or strike while you're concentrating on it. While you cannot ignore a knife or club, it is the wielder of the weapon, not the weapon itself, who presents the greatest threat to your well-being.

Once intimidating preliminary slashes are out of the way, an amateur will most likely use either a straight lunging stab or wide or tight slashes from side-to-side or from above or below. If you have the space to do so, such attacks can be evaded while kicking low to disable the knee.

Attempting high kicks for defensive purposes usually just gives the assailant an easy target in the form of the ankle and knee ligaments as well as the major arteries on the insides of the thigh. Similarly, most streetfighters expect and are prepared for a kick to the genitals.

While the movies and some martial arts instructors would have you believe that it is possible to kick or strike the weapon from the attacker's hand, such tactics are foolhardy in the extreme unless you've practiced them under all conditions and your attacker is an amateur.

Consequently, do your best to strike somewhere vital (e.g., throat, eyes), preferably while also attacking the joints of the arm holding the weapon. Remember that someone drunk or drugged is liable to be insensitive to pain as is someone "high" on adrenaline. Attacking the joints of the upper or lower body will force your opponent to cease using that arm to hold and direct the weapon or keep him from using his legs to pursue you.

Throw dirt, ashtrays, coins, a chair, or any object close at hand that could make the attacker blink or stumble even for a moment. When attempting to dodge a stab or slash, wait until the last possible moment before reacting, as this will lessen the attacker's opportunity to change the direction of a cut or stab suddenly.

Most of those who carry knives in the cities are cowards who need a weapon to bolster their courage, but don't let such motivations fool you. A weapon in the hand of a frightened man or woman is a potentially lethal threat, even to those with martial training.

CONCLUSION

Competent unarmed self-defense training should not just teach you physical skills but also how to understand your own fear so that it no longer controls how you react in the face of stress. True relaxation is difficult to achieve and is only tested when you are faced with someone who is really determined to hurt you—not a partner in a training setting.

What makes t'ai chi unique is that its self-defense skills can continue to mature despite the aging process, which plays havoc with skills based on speed and muscle alone. In addition, it improves your mental health and attitudes.

Unfortunately, finding an instructor who can balance a "playful" class atmosphere, combat "realism," and the safety of the students while training, in addition to transmitting the martial expression of t'ai chi skills, is, in some ways, the real challenge.

One option for those who wish to learn martial skills and cannot locate a competent or compatible t'ai chi teacher with such expertise is to learn a traditional *long* form and, in conjunction, practice a martial art whose theories and tactics approach those of t'ai chi.

The study of solo form, even when divorced from the interactive side, goes a long way toward helping a practitioner develop a holistic integrity through understanding the dynamics of balance, relaxation, and energy movement. Such a feeling, once internalized, can certainly be applied to other forms of martial expression.

For example, I have known many who have combined the study of aikido with that of t'ai chi with benefit to their understanding of each as expressions of a martial whole. It is true that, as a result of this process, you can become "neither fish nor fowl," which will displease the purists of both sides, but that is immaterial to whether or not you benefit from the training on an individual level.

CHAPTER 9

T'AI CHI AND MARTIAL CROSS-TRAINING

Conversely, experienced t'ai chi martial artists should consider cross-training, especially in those styles that have a philosophical similarity to our art. Such training helps to sharpen your self-defense skills through exposure to different tactics than those you are used to. In addition, it is good mental exercise to learn skills that have to be kept well-defined from those you have already developed.

For example, the study of pa-kua, another internal art, can help develop a broad range of tactical and theoretical skills that compliment rather than contradict those learned studying t'ai chi.

In the "old days," many internal experts were competent in styles of all three internal arts (hsing-i, pa-kua, and t'ai chi). Times have changed, and few of us have the time or the desire to devote ourselves to such skill attainment.

Today, it's a little more practical to think of studying the internal/external martial arts as being like attending a university. When working toward a liberal arts degree, you often have two main fields of study—a major and a minor.

If t'ai chi is your "major," then choosing a "minor" for cross-training purposes is complicated by factors like your age, physical condition, temperament, and amount of extra time, as well as the availability of qualified instructors.

The style you choose should also emphasize yielding and redirecting force rather than opposing force; self-defense; and the close, grappling range of most unarmed assaults, as these are essentials in the martial study of t'ai chi.

Keeping in mind the risk of being threatened by a knife or blunt instrument, it makes a great deal of sense to select a style that takes a realistic approach to defending against such weapons. Conversely, some styles overemphasize such weapons use and neglect effective unarmed techniques. Again, a balanced approach is preferable, even if difficult to find.

The following survey is not meant to be exhaustive. The martial arts listed are those I have experienced over the years which have been used by t'ai chi practitioners and instructors whom I respect and which are relatively available, at least in the urban centers.

Even though they share some common ground with the spirit of t'ai chi, I have excluded both Western and Thai kickboxing, amateur and professional wrestling, and judo, as these are rigorous competitive *sports* that are begun most easily when young.

In addition, those purposely excluded—like many of the hard styles—can be counterproductive for the t'ai chi form student. Such arts can make the student *less*, not more, relaxed and completely nullify the physical/emotional benefits of form practice. However, some of the tactics and techniques of these sports are certainly adaptable to t'ai chi principles when approached by the more experienced student.

With the exception of boxing and kali/escrima, the arts listed do not have competitive elements and can be practiced, at some eventual level of competence, by anyone in good health. The latter are also more suited to the younger, fit beginner.

Aikido

Developed in Japan in the 1930s and 1940s by the late Morehei Ueshiba, an expert in swordsmanship and a variety of styles of unarmed combat, aikido was refined and further developed by the founder's sons and senior students.

This martial art trains the practitioner to maintain an internal spiritual harmony despite being attacked. Returning rather than resisting aggressive actions is cultivated for emotional as well as martial ends.

The emphasis on learning how to roll and fall "softly" certainly minimizes the chance of injury from accidents or from being thrown and is by itself a desirable skill, as is the emphasis on locking joints and restraining as opposed to striking.

While its physical techniques include throwing and grappling by means of joint-locking, the art's emphasis is on training the student to psychologically "refuse" to participate in the attack being directed at him or her. Advanced practitioners seem to develop a psychic sixth sense of movement which seems to take them harmlessly through an aggressive action.

Old films of Master Ueshiba show him waiting serenely as burly karate students rush him from all sides at once. The next moment, he is standing beside a pile-up of the attackers who have collided over the spot he had occupied. Even when viewing these same films in slow-motion, it can be difficult to see the specific movements that take him safely out of the way of harm.

It is not surprising that such mastery led the less sophisticated to believe that Ueshiba was able to disappear and rematerialize at will. On a more mundane martial level, the action films of Steven Seagal, a high-ranking aikidoist, demonstrate, with some claim to realism, how this art can function in a self-defense context.

There are several styles currently being practiced, most of which emphasize the spiritual and integrative aspects of this art. Some instructors, however, have carried this to the extreme, and the attacks used during practice have become stylized, choreographed, and do not reflect the realities of the street.

Boxing

Western boxing as we know it has evolved from English bareknuckled sport matches which, for many years, were brutal (and illegal) endurance contests between fighters.

As a modern professional and amateur sport, boxing has become a contest in which the participants attempt to outhit each other by strategic punching. Physical conditioning as well as evasion through slipping, ducking, and footwork are the foundations of the sport. Depending on the preferences of the coach and fighter, the style can be aggressive or defensive.

As a self-defense and fitness system, boxing is excellent. However, as it is physically demanding even at the amateur level, it is a system suited more to the already physically fit. In addition, though gloves and headgear are used when training and a number of blows are prohibited, boxing as a full-contact sport is dangerous, especially for those who don't train seriously.

As blows to the head are common, the brain can suffer serious damage with potentially life-threatening implications from even moderate blows if enough of them are absorbed over time. At an amateur level, protective headgear is worn when sparring, but even this does not eliminate the cumulative effect of being struck to the head.

However, anyone with an appreciation of the principles of t'ai chi as a martial art can see the internal aspect in the sparring skills of someone like Sugar Ray Leonard or Mohammed Ali when those two were in their prime. Ali's eloquent "float like a butterfly and sting like a bee" allegory is one which aptly describes the soft and hard of t'ai chi.

William C.C. Chen of New York, whose foundation as an internationally respected t'ai chi instructor was his training with the father of North American t'ai chi, Cheng Man-ching, has had admirable success in adapting boxing tactics to fit the principles of t'ai chi.

Hsing-I/Pa-Kua

As with other martial arts, there is a bewildering and often contradictory variety of stories about the history of the other two internal martial arts.

Hsing-i is said to have been created by Yueh Fei, a famous Chinese general of the Sung Dynasty. Considered the oldest of the three, its practice was centered in the north of China in Shansi-Hopei and Honan provinces until recently. It has only been taught in the West in the last few decades.

The roots of pa-kua (chang) are in the deliberate obscurity of the Taoist temples. Tung Hai-ch'uan, the first public instructor in modern times at the turn of the present century, was renowned for his ability to adapt the principles of his art to the existing martial capabilities of his senior students.

Pa-kua chang literally means "eight diagram palms" and refers to the eight patterns of parallel lines used in the *I-Ching, The Book of Changes.* Most defensive/offensive movements are done with the open hand; kicks are low, and the footwork is precise and nimble.

The essence of this art is change—change of direction and tactic done while walking a circular pattern and executing, at a basic level, combinations of the eight different hand positions.

Early in the development of hsing-i and pa-kua, a tradition of encouraging their respective students to cross-train in both arts developed. It was obvious, then as now, that the skills learned were complementary and that the sum of the whole was greater than the two individual parts.

Traditionally, hsing-i was for the young, pa-kua for the middle-aged, and t'ai chi for the older martial artist, but the validity of this depends largely on the health of the *novice* and the variation of the style being studied.

Hsing-i is difficult to begin past the age of thirty-five, especially if the style being studied emphasizes "stamping" energy, which can be hard on the ankles and knees when executed improperly. It is based on the interaction of the Chinese Five Elements and on the practitioner's assimilating the "i" (mind or intention) that motivates the movements (the "form") of twelve birds and animals. Its five core actions (split, drill, crush, pound, and cross) are interrelated and form its tactical foundation. Hsing-i makes a more pronounced use of the fist than either pa-kua or t'ai chi.

Both arts, like t'ai chi, emphasize balance, natural breathing, and total relaxation; stability of stance without rigidity; the development of internal energy; the use of the waist/tan tien; and the use of the mind to create intent.

Like t'ai chi, both hsing-i and pa-kua come in a bewildering variety of styles and interpretations whose instructors are still relatively rare in North America. Their popularity is, however, growing rapidly and outstrips the supply of legitimate instructors.

Think of the energy movement in hsing-i as being like a roller-coaster moving up and down and (usually) straight ahead, that of pa-kua like a roller-coaster moving up and down on a circular track, and that of t'ai chi like a roller-coaster twisting freely in all directions.

Jeet Kune Do

The literal translation of this Chinese phrase jeet kune do (JKD) is "way of the intercepting fist," and the art was conceived by Bruce Lee in the late 1960s and early 1970s as a philosophical and intuitive approach to self-discovery through martial training.

Though it is often described as such, JKD is not just a composite system of techniques and principles taken from different arts. However, it can resemble Thai boxing, wing chun, wrestling, or kali/escrima, depending on the orientation of the instructor and the skills being demonstrated or used.

One of the key concepts of JKD is that students should learn through experience, not through blind repetition of an isolated set of tactics. For example, a boxer would be exposed to kicking techniques so that he could adapt his repertoire to dealing with those kind of attacks.

It is important to remember that JKD is not a defined style. The JKD "family" of instructors include such diverse talents as Dan Inosanto, Larry Hartsell, Jerry Poteet, and Richard Bustillo, and their training approaches vary quite widely.

Of particular relevance to those interested in t'ai chi are the training methods of Daniel Lee in California, who teaches JKD concepts but has also made a lifelong study of both t'ai chi and wing chun.

While most of the recognized instructors of JKD are in the United States, there are apprentice and certified instructors around the world.

In essence, JKD is primarily about absorbing what is useful to your training and martial needs while rejecting what is useless and adding something of your own. Such concepts are certainly compatible with those of t'ai chi.

Jujutsu

This is a generic term applied to numerous systems of Japanese combat, which are often completely different in terms of whether they are offensive or defensive in nature. It includes methods of kicking, striking, kneeing, throwing, choking, joint locks, and holds, as well as the use of, and defensive tactics against, a variety of bladed and blunt impact weapons.

The emphasis in many styles is on counterattacking, which makes it relevant to the defensive fighting skills to be developed according to the t'ai chi principles and classics in which the practitioner never, under normal circumstances, strikes first.

North American instructors and styles tend to be progressive and eclectic in that they are willing to incorporate techniques from other arts. Training emphasizes physical conditioning, learning how to fall safely, and practice of techniques designed to block, strike, and then follow up with a joint lock, choke hold, or throw. In most styles, little emphasis is put on form practice, the use of high kicks, or sport sparring. At the higher belt levels, practical unarmed defenses against weapons are taught.

Allan Weiss, my main instructor before I began teaching, had studied both jujutsu and aikido before coming to t'ai chi and always felt that his experience with those arts had helped his understanding of the principles of the art.

Kali/Escrima

These fighting arts from the Philippines have retained their combat realism since their origin in the sixteenth century and have become very popular around the world in the last two decades due to the efforts of several instructors, notably Dan Inosanto and Remy Presas.

These systems rely on speed of delivery, proper body position, and redirecting an attack rather than on size, strength, and head-on confrontation. Depending on the style, of which there are several, unarmed tactics will either predominate or be subordinate to the use of the knife, baton, sword and/or staff—either one at a time or one in each hand simultaneously.

A number of instructors emphasize defensive tactics of the single baton to parry all manner of knife, club, and hand attacks in conjunction with joint locks and restraints using the baton as a lever. As an interesting variation of the general approach in other martial arts, students usually learn to use weapons *first* and then train in unarmed techniques as a backup (i.e., if they are disarmed).

Most clubs and instructors teach only combat applications, but there has been a trend in the last few years toward competition sparring using protective armor. However, most styles continue to emphasize combative, as opposed to sporting, applications.

Wing Chun

A southern external style of kung fu, it is said to have been invented by a woman, Wing Chun ("Beautiful Springtime"), who gave her name to the style. Its most famous exponent in recent years was Yip Man of Hong Kong, who taught Bruce Lee in the latter's formative years as a martial artist.

An economical close-range self-defense system, wing chun emphasizes intercepting and redirecting incoming force, the use of aggressive and forceful sensitivity training called chi sau ("sticky hands"), a small number of forms that are done with relatively little footwork, and the use of "wooden dummies" to practice simultaneous trapping and striking tactics while conditioning the arms and legs.

A number of American instructors, notably James DeMile of Seattle, have modified traditional wing chun training to create their own eclectic and "modern" approaches to this art.

CONCLUSION

In the grand old days of t'ai chi, most of its best practitioners/instructors were men with a wide variety of martial experience. Unless you're a beginner at more than one thing at a time, your progress in each art is not likely to be hindered if you cross-train. However, there are still many instructors of both hard and soft styles who will refuse to teach you unless they feel that they have your undivided attention and loyalty.

Some t'ai chi instructors will refuse to teach even form if they know you are studying another martial art. This can be for reasons as varied as ethical prejudice against any type of martial practice, wanting to help you channel your energies, professional jealousy, or simply feeling that what they are offering is a complete approach.

You may have to withhold aspects of the truth about your situation and interests to gain access to some teachers. I don't advocate lying, but it isn't always necessary to volunteer information that hasn't been directly sought.

While trying to mix and match martial styles can have its own pitfalls for the practitioner, it is as true in the combative arts as it is in life that the more varied and extensive your experience, the better off you will be as a person in the long run.

If you feel somehow cheated by this short text because it describes aspects of t'ai chi that interest you without going into great detail, use that feeling of frustration to motivate your own training and research, preferably with the personal guidance of an instructor.

The study of the various sides of t'ai chi ch'uan is like being faced with a banquet of dishes—some plain and nourishing (form practice), others exotic and nourishing (the interactive aspects), others seemingly impressive but tainted with botulism or empty of food value (ch'i training to develop "power").

If you eat too much too soon, even of the nourishing dishes, you'll develop indigestion and be reluctant to return, even when hungry again.

If you rush from plate to plate, taking only a bite or two from each, you may lose your appetite before having the chance to fill yourself with something nourishing.

If you choose one dish prematurely, even if it's very nourishing, and eat only from it, you won't have room for any of the other

CONCLUSION

dishes. If you pick one that's tainted and continue to eat despite feeling that something isn't right, you'll sicken or die.

If you refuse to try dishes because of their appearance or your own preconceptions, you are summarily dismissing aspects that might be of benefit. The only way to know for sure is to take a bite—just be ready to spit out anything poisonous!

Ideally, learning t'ai chi ch'uan or any of the internal arts is a life-long process. Once the essential physical and emotional insights have been gained, ongoing instruction and physical practice are less necessary than they once were—as long as you don't allow complacency to take their place.

If you're a large carp in a pool of minnows, it's easy to feel that you know it all in terms of technical/spiritual proficiency. If you're a small carp in a pond full of bigger and exotic tropical fish, it's easy to lose sight of whatever proficiency you do possess and become disheartened. You should, by contrast, use the example of the more experienced and/or talented to spur your own growth process.

Aside from unarmed defense against the knife and club, I didn't discuss any aspects of traditional weapons training (spear/staff, sword, and saber), though such skills remain relevant even in the modern world with its preoccupation with "high-tech" weapons of mass and long-distance destruction.

This omission is not due to a lack of opinions on such training! Like many t'ai chi practitioners, I learned weapons forms very early in my training and practiced them for some years before stopping for over a decade. It is only in the last three years that I have resumed their practice and begun to understand how difficult it is to train safely and properly in their solo and interactive use.

Learning weapons forms and applications before you have an intuitive understanding of the principles of t'ai chi is counterproductive. Too many practitioners are content to do gymnastics and theater in the way of weapons forms, content to construct an attractive package that obscures the lack of substance within.

Learn the unarmed basics *first*; then, if your interests take you in that direction, refine your skills through weapons training—both form and function.

If there is a secret to overall competent or advanced t'ai chi development, it is to practice! Practice regularly, set realistic and moderate long-term goals for yourself, and periodically get back to basics in terms of your training schedule. Within reason, strive to make the art fit you, not you fit the art!

There are no aspects of t'ai chi ch'uan that cannot be learned, in the long run, through an enjoyment of the process for its own sake, hard work, and competent instruction.

Finally, practicing t'ai chi is a lot like making love. Even when you're a beginner, it's still very satisfying—as long as you put your heart and body in it.

Since 1980, Michael Babin has had more than ninety articles published in a variety of North American and international police and martial arts magazines (including *Official Karate*, *T'ai Chi Combat & Healing*, *Black Belt*, *Karate/Kung-Fu Illustrated*, *Inside Kung-Fu*, *Tai Chi*, *Law & Order*, *Trooper*, and *Police Review*. He also edited and contributed to a book on police survival skills (*Too Close for Complacency*, by Santiago & Mulroy, Sentel Publishing, 1990).

Born in 1952, Michael is married and the father of two sons. He has a university degree in the arts, as well as diplomas in counseling and journalism. He was a civilian writer/editor with the *RCMP Gazette*, a monthly Canadian police magazine, for ten years.

From 1975 to the present, he has earned rankings in styles of karate, jujutsu, taekwon do, and wing chun do, and studied elements of preying mantis, choy lay fut, jeet kune do, escrima, hsing-i, and pa-kua with a variety of instructors.

Beginning the study of t'ai chi ch'uan in 1975,

Michael trained without interruption for ten years, in particular with Steven and Shirley Choi and then Allan Weiss, before he began to instruct in 1985. Since that time, the main influences on his practice and teaching have been Erle Montaigue of Australia and William C.C. Chen of New York.

He teaches t'ai chi form to beginners on a contract basis with community and private fitness centers and the martial aspect to advanced students at his studio in Ottawa, Canada. The author's curriculum includes short and long yang forms; tui shou, da-lu, and small san sau; and weapons and self-defense.

He is an instructor in the World Taiji Boxing Association, headed by Erle Montaigue.